D1171358

HAPPY HIGH STATUS

www.penguin.co.uk

HAPPY HIGH STATUS

HOW TO BE EFFORTLESSLY CONFIDENT

Viv Groskop

torva

TRANSWORLD PUBLISHERS
Penguin Random House, One Embassy Gardens,
8 Viaduct Gardens, London SW11 7BW
www.penguin.co.uk

Transworld is part of the Penguin Random House group of companies
whose addresses can be found at global.penguinrandomhouse.com

First published in Great Britain in 2023 by Torva
an imprint of Transworld Publishers

A CIP catalogue record for this book
is available from the British Library.

ISBN 9781911709275

Typeset in 10.25/15pt Plantin MT Pro by Jouve (UK), Milton Keynes
Printed and bound in Great Britain by Clays Ltd, Elcograf S.p.A.

The authorized representative in the EEA is Penguin Random House Ireland,
Morrison Chambers, 32 Nassau Street, Dublin D02 YH68.

Penguin Random House is committed to a sustainable
future for our business, our readers and our planet. This book
is made from Forest Stewardship Council® certified paper.

To SPT

Contents

Picture yourself arriving at a post-Oscars party. Maybe you are a movie star. Or the greatest director since Kathryn Bigelow. Or a multi-award-winning writer. Or an extremely accomplished, ruthlessly competitive but ethically sound and morally responsible executive producer. You're late for this party because you were getting changed into your fourth fabulous outfit of the day in your hotel suite and the limo queue was hell. As you ascend the plushly carpeted stairs of the party venue and sweep through the doors, you feel a twinge of guilt that you've kept your A-list friends waiting. You can just about make out a crowd of them at the back of the room. As you rush across, slightly embarrassed for being so late, you absent-mindedly brush past a waiter near a tray of cocktails on the bar and, with your eyes fixed on your impatient friends, mutter something about him following you with a drink. You weave your way through the guests, sensing this waiter following behind you as requested. As you turn to take the drink from him before greeting your friends, your eyes lock when you see that the waiter is . . . George Clooney. That is to say, it is not a waiter at all but a fellow party guest wearing a tuxedo, whom you have mistaken for a waiter. It's potentially a very embarrassing error. But George's expression tells you it's OK. And, oh, how you laugh! 'It's an easy mistake to make,' he says, 'Not a big deal. Let me get a round in for your friends! Can I get you an olive with that?'

The look on George's face? You guessed it. Happy high status.

Yes, this is a fantasy and not a true story.

But happy high status is real. You know it when you see it.

And you don't have to be Clooney (or anywhere close) to get a piece of it.

Introduction

'What Is the Point of Happy High Status?' (Asked No Happy High Status Person Ever)

What Does Happy High Status Look Like?

Some people access a quality called happy high status – a kind of effortless confidence devoid of ego and self-consciousness – so easily that it's written all over their face. We all recognize those moments when we see them played out in front of us. It's the smile in President Volodymyr Zelenskiy's eyes when he's tirelessly reassuring the people of Ukraine in the wake of some new horror. It's the compassion in the voice of Jacinda Ardern, prime minister of New Zealand during the pandemic, when she's announcing – despite everything she promised before – a lockdown. It's the composure in comedian Chris Rock's posture as he glances off-stage while he's live at the Oscars and realizes that the show must go on and he needs to hurry up and announce the next award. It's the urgent, productive anger rising in Greta Thunberg at the podium at a summit of international leaders when she asks why she keeps having to deliver the same messages about the climate crisis. It's a quality that is immediately recognizable, easy to connect with and comes from a place of deep calm and unmistakable self-trust.

When a person is happy high status, they make us pay attention and convince us to believe in them, without us even having to think about it. The truly self-assured aren't focused on themselves. They're focused on making other people feel big and on making anything seem possible and manageable. But this quality of assurance is not just for extraordinary people in extraordinary circumstances. It is for all of us and in every walk of life.

Even if we don't have it right now, this state of being is easily summoned up. For most people, bringing to mind an emotionally positive moment, however fleeting, is achievable. Think of a time in your life when you felt great about something. Let's set the bar low with a single moment so that anyone can imagine it. It doesn't have to be monumental. It could be ordinary. It could have lasted a moment, a week or a year. Do please get in touch and let me know if you've succeeded in feeling that way for a year or more, by the way, because we need to become best friends as you appear to have it all worked out and it's probably you who should be writing this book, not me.

It's a sense of capability, confidence and self-belief. It's that inner conviction that you could do anything, that you've got this, that everything is going to be OK. For some people, it comes if they are on stage, in front of a crowd or in the spotlight, in that moment when they realize that things are coming together. For some, it's a moment of quiet satisfaction at work, the knowledge of a job well done. For others, it's at the end of a run or an exercise class when they feel a sense of elation and achievement. For a few of us, it might just be the sudden awareness that comes once a year when you wake up and you realize, having momentarily forgotten, that it's your birthday. It's a moment that gives you something close to joy, but not quite as overwhelming, like a fusion of awe and humility, like a sense of 'enoughness'. Now, just conjure up that feeling in yourself for a split second.

This feeling – the real you on a good day, full of capability, competence and devoid of self-doubt – is *happy high status*. What if we could be that person with that feeling a lot more often? What if we could use that feeling, which bubbles up, uncomplicated, when we're not under pressure, and harness it to use in situations when we really are under pressure? What if you could feel as comfortable giving a speech in front of hundreds of people as you feel when you're blowing out the candles on your birthday cake? *What if you could handle moments that make you feel sick with the same energy that you have on a day when you feel at your most relaxed?*

You might be thinking that it's just about being more 'confident'. But the term 'happy high status' is helpful here because the traditional definition of what we term as 'confidence' can be a stumbling block. Happy high status gives us interchangeable or alternative terminology that helps us to approach these kinds of questions: 'What do I mean by confidence? Why do I want to develop that quality? What would I use it for? How am I losing out by not having the confidence I want?' It's my hunch that a lot of people say they want to be more 'confident' because they think confidence is something we are *supposed to aspire to*. But they don't really want to do the work that might help them become more confident because they are cautious of repercussions. 'Confidence' has baggage. Become too confident and you might become insufferable. There's no denying that some people deemed 'confident' are just really annoying and overbearing. There's a comfort and a protection in making sure no one can ever accuse you of being one of them. Similarly, some people are genuinely overconfident. That can be a bonus, when they bring enthusiasm, optimism and excitement to the environment around them. But their actions can be ill-advised and reckless, bringing disaster. No one wants to be one of those people. It's difficult to find the happy medium. Especially when, annoyingly enough, trying to find it would appear to require the very confidence that we know we don't have right now.

Be confident according to your own definition

The truth is, we have an unnecessarily narrow and unhelpful definition of what confidence is and who has it. And we falsely correlate it with extroversion. Even if it was true in the past – that only the loud, ebullient and self-assured could find a platform (which in itself is debatable) – it's certainly not true now. Greta Thunberg, the Swedish climate activist, is the ideal contemporary example. For all her extraordinary effectiveness as a campaigner and public speaker, it's fair to say that she does not match up with a textbook nineteenth- or twentieth-century definition of 'confidence'. She does not have the gravitas of an old-school parliamentarian, the patter of a music-hall turn or the zinging smile of a Broadway chorus girl. In her own words: 'I've always been a shy, invisible girl at the back. I still do not understand why people listen to me.' Thunberg has Asperger's syndrome, a form of autism. She is softly spoken, has suffered from depression ('for three or four years') and was only fourteen when she first started speaking in public about climate crisis. It's no small thing either that, whenever she speaks in public, including live broadcasts and addressing stadium-sized crowds, she is doing so in a second language (her mother tongue is Swedish). Her influence is not as a result of being some kind of a curious prodigy: she has a global influence and reach because her message is heard and understood. There is something about her and the way she carries herself that represents a new kind of self-assurance: quiet, unassuming, the opposite of overbearing. This is happy high status: a confidence that is elastic, malleable, creative, surprising. It is unmistakable when we see it. And yet it will look different on everyone.

The trouble with our traditional understanding of the word 'confidence' is that it is often used to mean arrogance. To think about 'confidence' can feel intimidating: we don't always want to admit that we are confident even when we are. We might jinx it or people might judge us to be conceited. Happy high status as a term is freeing because it is open to interpretation and does not have these connotations. It is a feeling of ease that allows us to express ourselves in a way that does not feel forced or as if it's conforming to a standard. It is a conviction that lands upon you, independent of your own evaluation of yourself. It gets past your evaluation. It escapes your inner critic. Happy high status allows you to dwell in the calmness and contentment of just being. Imagine going for a job interview and someone asks you, 'Do you feel confident?' Already the question is loaded and terrifying. It makes you feel nervous. But if you can think, instead of *being confident*, of *channelling happy high status*, the whole affair becomes less fraught. Greta Thunberg doesn't think, 'I need to look confident.' She just lets herself be who she is. That is a more modern, twenty-first-century broadening of the definition of confidence. It's so individual that it may well look, on everyone who tries it out, like something that we have never seen before.

Happy high status is a strange expression – and we'll get to understanding why it's called that, and exactly what it encompasses – but it is not dependent on us thinking that we're the greatest, or even on anything that involves our intellect or our self-judgement. It is presence, equanimity, grounded optimism, openness, ease. It is a feeling that we can access at almost any time and use to give ourselves strength and energy. It's a sort of everyday, ordinary superpower that the greatest performers, speakers and leaders channel effortlessly, without even realizing it. It's a key quality of leadership and the ultimate life tool. It has something to do with a lack of self-consciousness (because you are thinking more of others than you are of yourself) and it has a lot to do with the quietening of the ego (because it's a reduction in self-importance).

It's important to underline the versatility of this resilient, flexible kind of confidence. It's not just something that happens on good days or when you're 'winning', or when everyone is applauding you. It can also be used amidst chaos, disaster and failure. Think of the case of the Chris Rock incident, for example, when the comedian was presenting an award at the 2022 Academy Awards. When he was struck across the face on stage by the actor Will Smith during a live broadcast, Rock's reaction was governed purely by an instinct familiar to anyone who has worked as a comedy MC or event host. No matter what happens, you stay in control, you remain the anchor point, you retain the focus of the room. His reaction was a sort of in-the-moment ego-free non-reaction that allowed him to step back and get on with the job. You could argue that he should have reacted differently. Perhaps you think he should have punched Will Smith back or that he should have angrily taken charge and called for the producers to cut the live feed. But instead the reaction he chose – 'the show must go on' – was temperate, generous and – though he had only a micro-second to get to this decision – considered. This was a subjective, personal response but he was able to 'sell' it as the right thing for everyone. That is happy high status.

As I've suggested, this kind of confidence is not a singular way of being and it does not look the same on everyone. Chris Rock and Greta Thunberg are not remotely similar. The way they project confidence is going to be completely different. Which makes sense when you think about it, because everyone's version of 'I've got this' is going to look different and is going to be used to achieve different goals. I do not expect Greta Thunberg to be hosting the Oscars any time soon and I'm sure she's pretty happy about that. And I doubt Chris Rock is interested in reinventing himself as a climate activist. Happy high status is defined by the character and the interests of the person channelling it. It's the confidence of a semi-silent introvert who persuades with well-placed arguments. It's the confidence of someone who dislikes crowds and noise, and so seeks to influence one-to-one. It's the confidence of a performer who can mesmerize one second and share the limelight with someone equally mesmerizing the next. It's true that happy high status is sometimes best explained by using examples from the entertainment world, from politics, from sport or from popular culture. But that is only because those examples are easily pictured. Just because exemplary confidence is easily evidenced in those areas of life, it doesn't mean it is confined to those areas. You can borrow ideas of confidence from anywhere and apply them for your own ends in your own world, whatever kind of person you are.

This is not about being perfect or even especially 'happy'

Happy high status is not about perfection, getting it right every time and never experiencing a low moment. Neither is it about being literally 'happy' all the time (not least because it pays to be deeply mistrustful of anyone who says they are happy all the time). And it is not about having the kind of status that is conferred by the social *status* of political power, wealth, job titles or a gilt-edged business card. Sorry to say that it is also not about getting *high*. That's a completely different set of instructions. It is the confidence that persists even when you are supposedly 'unhappy', made sober by the vicissitudes of life and/or forced into a position of supposed low social status. It is more about managing difficulty, unpredictability and anxiety, and about the business of coping with situations that are not of our choosing, than it is about channelling some kind of fake positivity. To give an extreme example, Zelenskiy's situation could not be further from his choosing and has been largely out of his control. And yet he maintains an equilibrium that makes people listen and inspires trust. It is about pragmatism and honesty. We cannot be confident all the time. But we can almost always inhabit the ease of internal equilibrium, even when the external conditions are dire.

So if this state is so easy to inhabit, then why don't we fall into it naturally and effortlessly? The simple answer is that ego gets in the way, usually in the form of self-protection, risk-avoidance, playing it safe, pre-empting negative judgement from others, or wishing that we were in control when we're not. We panic, and we think, 'Hmm, I thought I had this. But I really do not have this.' Arguably this might well be why birthdays are not a moment of happy high status for everyone. For some people, judgement creeps in: 'I'm older and that's a bad thing.' For some, comparison: 'Last year's birthday was better.' For others, it's about bad memories: 'Previous birthdays have been bad. This one probably will be too.' Once these negative thoughts have even crossed our mind, happy high status has taken a hike.

Judgement is the strongest enemy of happy high status. The one thing connecting people like Volodymyr Zelenskiy, Greta Thunberg, Chris Rock and Jacinda Ardern is that in difficult moments they can hold their own but they are not universally liked for it. They have their detractors, as does any human being, whether famous or unknown. Some people even have haters, maybe even millions of haters. Still, they can be happy high status, even if their version of self-assurance (and what they use it to achieve) is not appreciated by everyone. Their critics do not make their sense of ease and self-confidence any less real. A common misperception – or at least a secretly held belief – about confidence is that it makes you unassailable (no one is unassailable), that it makes you universally popular (no one is universally popular) and that it protects you from criticism (nothing can do this). If we can get past some of these myths and dig into the habits and behaviours that foster this new kind of confidence – both internally, in terms of how we regard ourselves, and externally, in terms of how others see us – then we have a stronger chance of strengthening and channelling this feeling and showing up as happy high status more often in life. Notice 'more often' rather than 'all the time'. No one can be rock-solid self-assured all the time.

This is a new way of thinking about confidence that is practical and not theoretical, actionable and not daunting. It is a fun – and sometimes sort of funny – way of thinking about confidence. It's worth treating your attitude to your own confidence with levity, as serious quests tend to become difficult and intimidating for us and then they become easy to abandon. But that's not to say that this fun endeavour isn't of importance. This is no frivolous under-taking, because the business of confidence is vital in addressing so many of the issues that are holding people back in their daily lives. We all deserve the ability to access our confidence whenever we need it. Identifying what it means to you to be happy high status and channelling that feeling as much as you can is at the heart of a meaningful, fulfilled and less troublesome life. And, goodness knows, life can be extremely troublesome at times. There's a deeper resonance here, too. Many kinds of people – from the self-labelled shy and introverted to those who feel mar-ginalized or ignored, right through to people who see themselves under-represented – too frequently count themselves out of opportunities because of their own per-ceived lack of confidence. Many have bought the myth that this nebulous gift of confidence buys you permission to do particular things, to occupy a given space, to enter a room. And if you don't have that gift? Well, you had better not knock on the door. This is the myth that stops people from stepping up to take power or to put themselves forward for leadership roles. But it's just that: a myth. It's time to put it to bed.

But lots of people seem to be successful *without* happy high status . . .?

There are many examples of 'success', 'leadership' and 'confidence' that would appear to contradict the principles of the sort of touchy-feely happy high status I'm describing. Granted, it's not the only way to move through the world. You can also use any combination of the following: high status (including bloody miserable high status), fear, threats, sheer will . . . Wealth, political rank and royal primogeniture would also help. You get the picture. Many popular and indeed many populist leaders do not need happy high status or anything close to it. They are living their best life very happily, even ecstatically, without it. And they have millions of supporters. Leaders like Donald Trump and Vladimir Putin really don't need my help or advice. (And I think it would be quite problematic to get them to take it.) Nor does anyone who you wouldn't want to mistake for a cocktail waiter, as in that George Clooney fantasy. You might have worked with someone with a short fuse who would take offence in a situation like that. Most of us have.

I don't want to suggest for a moment that these people are 'unsuccessful' in their fields of endeavour or that you can only get by in life by being open and forgiving. Often people who are aggressive and unyielding clearly and demonstrably achieve what they set out to achieve. How we decide to exercise power and move through the world is highly subjective. But it's easy to see the distinction between this kind of 'top down', dominating, unsubtle, non-collaborative power – which is not so much confidence as the use of force, whether it's literal force (or the threat of it) or force of personality – and a more enlightened, less old-fashioned, more nebulous kind of power that governs by consensus, by permission, by kindness, by altruism. I can see why that second kind of power – which is the essence of true confidence and requires no violence or exercise of force – would be unattractive and unwelcome to people who want to push through certain ideas and who find dissent and contrasting views unacceptable. So I am not suggesting that the ideas in this book are perfect for everyone. Or that they are the only way to do things. There's no point in sounding the death knell for the alpha ways. They will always have their allure. But today we live in a society that accommodates alternative ways of doing things. Happy high status allows you to push that fact to its limits.

There are many ways to exercise power, seek leadership and show confidence that we have not really seen yet as they have not been tried. Looking for a confidence handbook about the exercise of old-school power using the force of your personality alongside an army of mercenaries? Be my guest. Most history books have got you covered. We know how that stuff works, inside out. What we don't know so much about is a more subtle approach, one that feels new, raw, more authentic, messier and involves experimenting, one that comes from you personally and is not a carbon copy of something that has come before.

This second kind of power borrows an idea from the creativity of artists. If you think of almost any cultural contribution you've really enjoyed – from a musical to a song to a piece of visual art to a documentary – it's almost always the case that you couldn't have guessed in advance that you wanted that thing. There was some kind of magic and serendipity that occurred. You couldn't have named it in advance and it couldn't have been made to order. I'm thinking, for example, of the last TV show I loved: *The White Lotus*. I wasn't sitting around thinking, 'What I really need in my life right now is a brilliant drama about wealthy people bitching at each other in a beautiful hotel. I wonder where I can find that thing? Who will create that for me?' Instead that thing landed in front of me and I suddenly realized it was exactly what I needed, without knowing it. It's the same emotion when you hear a voice you love or a song lyric that connects with you. You weren't looking for it. You didn't 'order' it or 'predict' it. It just appeared and you knew it felt right.

What if great confidence comes from an equally surprising, creative, unplanned and unexpected place?

Artistic and cultural contributions emerge from trust, inspiration, experimentation and often a place of fun. They are about invention and curiosity. 'What if we tried this?' 'What if this works?' 'Wouldn't it be fun if . . .?' The results are not fixed and predictable. They don't always work. Not everyone loves the result in the same way. It strikes me that the expression of our greatest confidence is similar to this. Happy high status is not a cardboard-cut-out, made-to-order replica of our 'best self'. It's not a one-size-fits-all model of human confidence. It's a true artistic expression of who you really are. It's as flexible, adaptable, individual, original and subjective as any work of art.

How to use this book

Happy high status is about attitude and mindset. The stories, examples and theories mentioned here are intended to help you think differently about what confidence is and to examine how you might rethink your own definition of it. It can be surprising to realize that confidence is not something you learn from others or that lands upon you once you've studied it hard enough. It's something that's already within you that you summon up. You're probably already doing it in a lot of situations without defining it as confidence. If you can identify when that's happening and transfer that quality into any situation consciously and liberally . . . Job done.

Each chapter looks at a way of rethinking confidence

and explores a variation on happy high status (vulnerable, entertaining, dominant, balanced, generous, 'What if . . .?', 'leader', athletic and finally your own happy high status). Throughout each of the chapters and in the variation notes that follow ('Inspiration for . . .') are examples of well-known figures who have a flavour of that quality. These aren't fixed 'types' nor are they a suggestion that any individual conforms uniquely to any type. This is not a prescription or a recipe. The variations are guidelines and the celebrity examples are purely to help you visualize what this elusive quality of happy high status looks like on some people. And to act as a reminder that it's subjective: you won't 'like' all the people or want to 'be like them'. But hopefully you can see how their happy high status works for them. The variations are not meant to be like star signs or personality types, where you fit into one of a fixed number of options. They're suggestions, hints, jumping-off points. For example, I personally gravitate most easily towards the idea of 'entertaining' happy high status: I value the qualities of warmth, fun, making people laugh, putting people at ease. But I'm also really interested in 'athletic' happy high status. Even though I am not remotely sporty and am not going to trouble the International Olympic Committee any time soon, I find inspiration in that mindset: grace in defeat, noble failure, learning how not to be a sore loser. My aim in this book is to provide a wealth of examples so that you can find the people, ideas and behavioural models that inspire you.

The advice sections at the end of each chapter include

questions and tips to find the variation that will work for you. A lot of the thinking exercises are focused on finding confidence for moments when we face the scrutiny of others, whether that's for work meetings, for public speaking, for pitching, for arguing your corner, for persuading on a large scale or a small scale. There are two sides to confidence: the internal (how you feel about yourself) and the external (what others see). These two sides interact. If you strengthen your external presentation by behaving more confidently, dropping 'low status' body language cues and looking more relaxed, then – surprise, surprise – you shift your own internal perception: 'Oh, I really can do this.' And once you start to think and feel that internally, you adopt a more relaxed external presentation naturally anyway . . . It's a virtuous circle. The external picture feeds the internal confidence and vice versa. My job here is to help you grow both sides of confidence – external and internal – at the same time, so that the final effect is as effortless as possible.

Is this 'faking it till you make it'? 'Fake it till you make it' certainly sounds like a good idea. And if that works for you, then great. The trouble is, we all know that we can read 'fake' from a mile off. If 'fake it till you make it' really worked, everyone would already be as confident as they wanted to be. When your internal perception ('I am as confident as I need to be and without pretending to be something I'm not') matches your external projection ('Other people can see I'm OK with myself'), there's no mistaking it. Rather than faking it completely, here I suggest you try on different versions of confidence and find out what feels right to you. These tips and tricks offer suggestions that can be adapted to your own style. This is about experimentation and about making revisions and tweaks, rather than going all-out in pretending to be something you're not.

The main aim of the exercises is to help you understand yourself better. I want you to wean yourself off the idea that someone has the magic secret to confidence, and if only you can find out what it is, you can copy them. You'll find these practical tricks and exercises at the end of each chapter under the seemingly throwaway, but covertly indicative heading 'How to get a piece of it'. Aiming nonchalantly for 'a piece of it' serves as a reminder to keep it light and lower the stakes. It's about capturing a state of mind and adapting this version of confidence for yourself – not about being perfect and getting cross with yourself when things go wrong.

The point is to challenge our conventional ideas of what we think of as 'confidence' by redefining it as 'happy high status'. That gives you a neutrality and a fresh start. As a performance coach, I've tackled this subject face-to-face with people when they're doing something stressful that they think requires confidence (like preparing to host an event or talk in public). I've found that our preconceptions about this scary word 'confidence' get in the way. We think we should be acting, behaving, feeling, looking and speaking a certain way in order to be perceived as 'confident'. Usually this isn't even true and what we think of as 'confidence' is actually robotic, cold pseudo-perfectionism or just reads as bravado or fakery. We end up putting ourselves under enormous pressure to achieve something that isn't even valuable or necessary. In fact, this pursuit of confidence – which is really the pursuit of the confidence of an imaginary, non-existent person who is better than us – is potentially damaging. Real confidence is sometimes doing things well, sometimes doing things badly, but always doing them like a real, flawed human being. And one who harnesses their confidence according to their own values and according to what is immediately needed around them in their personal or professional life, in their company, in their team, in their family, in their community.

Chapter 1

BE LIKE THE TWENTY-FIRST-CENTURY HUMAN YOU ALREADY ARE

NO PERSONALITY TRANSPLANT REQUIRED

Vulnerable Happy High Status:
Inner Calm

Why listen to me?

I wish I could say that I am a person who has suffered from cripplingly debilitating low self-esteem my whole life and then suddenly, in a flash, I saw the light and now I am going to share the secret to flipping that switch overnight. Because wouldn't that be a great story? Unfortunately it is not the case. I come across as confident in public, even though in private I can occasionally be anxious and depressed. From year to year during my adult life I have been in weekly therapy more often than not. But I would not describe my problems as serious or clinical. Like anyone, I've held myself back at times, but mostly I've muddled through. My story is more that I was a moderately confident person – perhaps better able than most to fake confidence when necessary – and, over a long period, I learned how to become a more lavishly confident person most of the time, without faking it. I learned how to be just vulnerable enough, while remaining secure. And I learned to find an inner calm, without losing energy and drive. This is not a huge transformation, but a significant one. And one involving increasingly less fakery and a big dose of realism, instead of some kind of mental health happy-ever-after. (Although a tiny bit of fakery to get you through is only natural from time to time.) This is the kind of transform-ation that is worth aiming for: one that takes a while but is lasting – and is not so overwhelming that it scares you. It's a transformation that is real and – life's usual knockbacks and surprises notwithstanding – permanent.

I did, however, do one unusual and rare thing that fast-tracked my experience and has made me obsessed with confidence. It has also encouraged me to explore the myths we harbour about it, which hold us back in all kinds of ways. In my late thirties, ten years ago, I switched from being a journalist to being a stand-up comedian. It's true that while I have never been a shy and retiring person, I would not have had the confidence to do this earlier in my life, and it was only when I was approaching forty that I was able to channel some kind of *carpe diem* feeling and really do the thing I had always wanted to do. That led to a lot of things I never could have imagined embarking on: six years of Edinburgh shows, writing and performing in plays, being on TV and radio, and having up-close access to a lot of people who would seem, at face value, to have truly nailed it. Incidentally, if you are thinking, 'Why on earth would anyone do stand-up if they have a history of anxiety and depression?', then you have clearly not met very many comedians.

In the course of all this, I have become a sort of keen investigator and sometimes reluctant practitioner of flawed confidence: an ambassador for happy high status.

I say 'flawed' and 'reluctant' on purpose because one of the most important lessons to learn immediately is a painful one: no one is 100 per cent confident all the time. We all wish we could wave a magic wand and never have a moment of insecurity or pain. But we all have bad days and we all make bad decisions. However counter-intuitive it may sound, genuine confidence is in recognizing that sometimes we are going to be at the heart of a really rubbish situation of our own making. It is also in recognizing that our perception of success and failure, and what that does to our confidence, is often academic. The real evidence as to whether we have succeeded or not is not always apparent until long after the event. We should be cautious of letting our confidence hinge on our performance.

A basic illustration of this is a life event that is commonly regarded as one of the biggest knocks we can take to our confidence: losing a job or being made redundant. This is a horrible thing, a terrible shock, a real blow to your self-esteem. But after a period of time and with hindsight, many people will admit that moment was 'the best thing that ever happened' to them. A disastrous loss can turn out to be a blessing in disguise. The opposite is also true: a confidence-boosting win can turn out to be a poisoned chalice. This is the challenge of confidence, and it's summed up in the poem 'If' by Rudyard Kipling: 'If you can meet with Triumph and Disaster/And treat those two impostors just the same ...' We all know this, really. But instead of examining the complexity and confusion that dichotomy can conjure up, and acknowledging that often we can't tell the difference between 'success' and 'failure' until considerable time has passed, we tell ourselves fake stories about confidence and how if only we had more of it in our lives, everything would be perfect.

There are two parts to this work that we all need to do. The first lies in recognizing that we might have an out-dated, unworkable or historically irrelevant concept of what 'confidence' is, and that it might be more useful to think openly and creatively about what authority, gravitas and self-assurance look like in the twenty-first century. This makes more sense than trying to recreate models of behaviour and leadership from the past. Second, we need to realize that it is a total waste of time trying to 'be like' anyone else. Happy high status is not about imitating or emulating. Instead it's about drawing inspiration and asking, 'How do they do that?' Not so you can do the exact-same thing yourself. But so that you can work out how you might tailor it to your own style.

This exploration of happy high status is an intensely individual thing that will require you to think about how you show up. So it's not about trying to *copy* anyone else, least of all the author of this book, who is sometimes a total idiot. That said, I am qualified to be your guide on this mission, and although this is not about my personal experience and individual transformation, it is informed by those things. For the past five years I have run a pod-cast on performance and presence called *How to Own the Room*, inspired by my book of the same name. These two projects opened up a channel to thousands of readers' and listeners' innermost thoughts about their insecurities and stresses. The conversations on the podcast – mostly with women – are public because they are for broadcast, but all the same they are often vulnerable, exposing and intimate. With readers and listeners, at workshops, live events and online, I've had both public and private con- versations where I have learned what many of us, in our darkest moments, really think about confidence. The feedback I've heard has both inspired and disturbed me. Admittedly, I usually hear from a self-selecting group of people – men and women – interested in improving how they come across. I don't tend to hear from people who already feel that they're super-confident. Those people already think they can own the room without thinking about it. Instead, I get the raw stuff and I get it from both ends of the spectrum: successful transformation (people who have largely overcome their issues with their confi- dence) and ongoing trauma (people who can't seem to get to grips with their insecurities or find the same problems recurring from year to year or job to job).

To my delight, I have heard many positive accounts of people who have managed to challenge the self-limiting sob stories we so pointlessly feed ourselves, and who have taken small, manageable, consistent action in the right dir- ection, sometimes with life-changing effects. Often these successful experiments combine an awareness of that need for controlled vulnerability (taking risks, admitting mis- takes, opening up) with a sort of inner calm (avoiding showboating, not faking confidence, listening as much as talking). Equally, to my dismay, I have heard miserable stories of people who turned their back on careers they loved, which had delighted them for years, simply because they were asked to do more public speaking or take on a more public-facing role and their confidence just wasn't up to it. Worse, if you probe deeper in these cases, it almost always turns out that they were *the only person* who doubted themselves. Very rarely do people offer you prominent opportunities or encourage you to take up the spotlight if you are genuinely terrible at it and/or you make other people feel uncomfortable. Indeed it's often others who believe in our confidence more than we do. The fact is, I have seen that lasting and significant change is possible and not that difficult. And I have seen how many people desperately need to know how to do it.

Too many people believe they are not confident – with no real evidence to back up this belief

Our own perception of our confidence affects every aspect of our lives. And many people appear to be labouring under the misapprehension that if only they were confident in a certain bulletproof way all their problems would disappear. But cast-iron confidence is an illusion. It is flawed confidence that makes us human. Perversely, the more you accept that confidence is not supposed to feel like a certainty, the more you will project actual confidence. I realize this makes no sense but bear with me. Confidence is something people beat themselves up about – and in doing so they wreck whatever confidence they had in the first place. It's the perfect self-sabotage.

I meet so many people who are hostages to the thought 'If only I were more confident . . .' They will admit that they are avoiding doing certain things, almost waiting to become more confident and simply delaying their life. Sometimes that feeling of unease or 'I can't' is deeper than an idea or a self-perception and there's a physiological or medical root. Sometimes it happens to us for unavoidable circumstantial reasons, temporary or permanent. For example, you are not going to have an easy relationship with confidence if you grew up in an environment where you were constantly criticized. Similarly but with lesser long-term effects, you're not going to be feeling great if you've just been rejected from a third job interview in a row. There are often concrete reasons we can point to. And it can help to be specific if you know the origins of self-doubt.

But there are also less obvious sources of insecurity when our self-concept clings on to certain deeply held illusions – usually referred to, in self-help circles, as 'self-limiting beliefs' – that are holding us back for no good proven reason. This latter phenomenon can become a fact of life. The philosopher and psychologist William James, one of the founders of Harvard's Psychology department, called it 'the restricted circle' of our potential being. These self-limiting beliefs are less obvious to us than our

circumstances or life's ups and downs. Instead we incorporate them into the story of who we 'can't help being'. If
our early life was difficult, we might think, perfectly reasonably and usefully, 'I have a tendency to be too hard on
myself sometimes because I grew up in an unsupportive
environment.' Our self-limiting beliefs, though, are usually
more *unreasonable* and are expressed as generalizations:
'I'm rubbish at maths.' 'I'm terrible with money.' 'I've
never been good with people.' When we are experiencing
a dip in confidence – or a long-lasting dent – it's worth
picking apart these different strands and figuring out
which are relevant to us. (And if you are thinking, 'But,
Viv, I really am rubbish at maths, terrible with money and
can't stand people . . .', then I would argue that these things
might be true occasionally in some instances and on some
days, but it's highly unlikely that they are true all the time
in every sector of anyone's life.)

Confidence as a concept is ill-defined. We cannot see it
and yet we can feel it in ourselves. Sometimes we feel it
strongly and it's undeniable. At other times it is momentary
and fragile. And yet we believe that we can see it on display
in others. Although – and here's another contradiction – it is
not so obviously visible that everyone agrees on its proven
existence in a given individual. As we'll see throughout this
book, some people may argue that the confidence of certain
personalities in high office or at the helm of certain corpor-
ations is obvious, visible and incontrovertible. Others might
not see what those individuals have as 'confidence' and
might see it as another quality entirely, such as narcissism,

delusion or – let's be generous – misplaced confidence. Confidence is nebulous and subjective.

Neuroscience is beginning to understand confidence and demonstrate where and how it shows up in our brains. But most of the research on the prefrontal cortex, commonly understood to be the 'brain centre for confidence', is not about the kind of confidence most of us would like to have (the confidence that allows us to give a great talk, to ask someone out on a date or to ask for a pay rise). The prefrontal cortex – the confidence-influencing part that can be measured – is about perceptual awareness and what is known as 'decision confidence' – when your brain decides whether or not you have the confidence to cross the road right now. That's the kind of confidence most of us take for granted, thank goodness. The other kind, the subjective kind, is much harder to pin down. Happy high status is not a motor skill: it is an instinct you wouldn't be able to measure in a lab.

Despite that, one of the reasons I am personally gripped by this idea is because it forms a part of our mental well-being and self-worth that we can actually affect relatively easily. We may not be able to physically measure or quantify it, but we can influence it. I do not mean this in the wishy-washy sense of 'manifest your way to greatness by harnessing your inner vibrations'. (I feel like someone on Instagram has encouraged me to do that this very morning, using those exact words.) There are limits to how we can affect our own confidence. And when plummeting self-esteem becomes long-term self-neglect, self-loathing or mental illness, we've gone way beyond our own influence and we need help. But at the more manageable end of things, there are basic tips and tricks anyone can use to train themselves to maintain this sort of equilibrium, many of them borrowed from stagecraft, comedy and basic observation of human behaviour.

A key motivator for me in wanting to encourage more people to think about this concept is that I have encountered so many people who have a warped view of their own confidence and are suffering from self-doubt and hesitation *when there is absolutely no reason for them to feel that way*. When I say 'Be like the twenty-first-century human you already are', I mean that deep down, most people have more confidence than they think. They are already OK. They usually have reactions and instincts that are appropriate and proportionate in the modern world. But instead of appreciating the amazing good in themselves while gently admitting their weaknesses (vulnerable happy high status) and transferring the ease they have in some situations to life's more challenging moments (inner calm), they convince themselves that they're not good enough as they are and/or that they need to reach some mythical standard of behaviour (and one that may not even be relevant nowadays). They hold themselves back from difficult situations.

I facetiously call this But-I'm-Not-Winston-Churchill syndrome, which is a bombastic way of describing the tendency we can all sometimes have of counting ourselves out of things that feel daunting or scary. In order to justify our fear, we convince ourselves that we do not have the self-belief, the bravado, the public-speaking skills, the whatever ... without asking whether those attributes are really required. And without asking whether it's really true that we don't have those things in some measure. No one wants Winston Churchill back anyway. (And I'll explain in more detail in a later chapter how our perception of 'appropriate leadership' changes and becomes more elastic over time.)

Instead of appreciating the strengths they have and worrying less about who and what they're not, many people waste their time, energy and precious reserves of sanity on what I call 'non-problems': imaginary hurdles, insecurities over habits that are either relatively harmless or invisible to others, perceived inadequacies of all kinds. Many people believe that others can sense that they're not confident when they can't. Many have hang-ups about their voice or their accent or their posture or their articulacy that are purely in their own minds. Others have strange, unevidenced beliefs about the standard that must be attained in order to attempt certain things. To quote Michelle Obama on her reaction to being around elite types 'at every powerful table you can think of', once you get there, she said, you realize: 'Here's the secret: they're not that smart.'

These 'non-problems' often emerge because people think they need to be smarter or better – or more like a twentieth-century caricature of a 'strong leader' – when all they really need to do is become less self-conscious and more secure in their own strengths. I'm not being judge-mental about 'non-problems' or about the very common tendency to think that you're 'not good enough', because I've fallen into all those traps myself. But as Mrs Obama suggests, all of that is such a waste of time for no good reason.

Disclaimer: Might you need more support than you can get from reading a book?

The more serious reason for treating this topic as urgent is that many people from all walks of life are in pain. It has become something of a well-worn cliché over the past ten years to talk about a 'global mental health crisis'. This was a much-used phrase long before the pandemic. But since the pandemic, it has become all the more accepted as a fact of life. Many of the statistics linked to this area of research come from the US, where the Centers for Disease Control and Prevention reported in 2021 that 41.5 per cent of US adults 'exhibited symptoms of anxiety and depression'. Globally, a Gallup poll in early 2021 found that seven out of ten people were 'struggling or suffering'. This was at the height of the pandemic, when anxiety was not only understandable and often rationally justified but also being widely discussed and reported. These problems persist, pandemic or not. Although I do take some of these statistics with a pinch of salt. If someone came up to me in the street and asked me if I was 'struggling', my answer really would depend on how much caffeine I'd had on that day. Struggling or suffering by whose metric? Compared with what? Diagnosed by whom?

Nonetheless, these issues are genuine, alarming and widespread. They are more easily identified, named and diagnosed than they were decades ago. There is less stigma. And many people lead complicated and pressured lives where they have no access to the comforts of community or calmness. Health systems in many countries are ill-equipped to deal with mental health issues. Many people live with increasing financial pressure, whether that's literal and caused by poverty, or psychological and caused by the toxic comparisons encouraged in late-stage capitalism. Don't worry, I'm not going full-on Marxist, but it's really worth mentioning that a lot of superficial issues of confidence are caused by comparing ourselves negatively and unnecessarily with others, a tendency which has only increased during our lifetimes.

The pandemic has been widely viewed as exacerbating a problem that was already dire. In 2022 the United Nations secretary general António Guterres referenced a 'global mental health crisis' and announced that 1 billion people around the world now have a mental health issue. That's one in seven of us. These things would, sadly, not be taken as seriously if they were not accompanied by an estimate of the financial cost: 'Depression and anxiety alone cost the global economy an estimated 1 trillion US dollars per year,' said Guterres. Of course, the human cost matters more than the money. But a trillion is a thousand billion. Or, if that's hard to get your head around, a million million. That number is an attempt to express a human cost that is impossible to quantify.

This is not a book about the treatment of depression, anxiety or mental illness, because you need to see a qualified doctor for those conditions. But it is written in the context of our growing awareness of the importance of nurturing our self-esteem. A British GP interviewed in the *Guardian* in 2022 expressed the make-up of his patients like this: 'Classic mental health issues such as psychosis, bipolar disorder . . . that is probably 3 or 4 per cent of the people we see. Everything else is related to external stress or anxiety.' In other words, around 96 or 97 per cent of patients are presenting with mental health problems that are not to do with mental illness per se but more to do with the impact of their environment. And these are the ones who are actually going to see the doctor. There is a whole other sector of the population suffering with external stress and anxiety who are not seeing anyone. Confidence – and a reframing of it, using an idea like happy high status – is not the only solution. But if you can keep your self-view buoyant and flexible at a time when you recognize that your mental and emotional health is relatively good, then you're creating habits that will give you some protection from stress and anxiety, or at least make it easier for you to see things in proportion.

This, then, is about looking after our mental fitness and examining our day-to-day reactions, as long as we can still just about count ourselves among the six out of seven who the UN secretary general is not presently worrying about – and who aren't going to their GP. It is my instinct that the six out of seven of us who are 'not struggling or suffering' are nonetheless prone to a combination of low-level stressors that affect confidence: disrupted sleep, worrying in vague terms about worry itself, overworking and over-stressing, obsessing about what hybrid work really means, panicking that we either spend too little or too much time on social media, fretting that we don't have enough friends or that we need to spend more time 'networking' (whatever this is) and trying to decide if we have imposter syndrome (whatever that is). Most of the time that kind of thinking is manageable, if burdensome. When it becomes unmanageable, it can tip into depression and anxiety. Asking yourself what your version of happy high status is *when you are in a calm and collected state and figuring out what you can do to stay there more often* is one way of maintaining your mental and emotional fitness.

But when you are not in a calm and collected state, you need to undertake other courses of action. The ideas, suggestions and cheerleading in the guise of intelligent, questioning, practical self-help in this book are not a substitute for medical intervention. I want to hammer this home early on. I am a writer and a comedian, not a mental health professional. And this book is not intended as a replacement for therapy, counselling or any other kind of treatment. There are times in our lives when we need a pick-me-up, a pat on the back and someone in our corner. If that sounds about right, then welcome. But there are times in our lives when we really need expert help, time out or medication. Some challenges in our lives can be solved with the sort of advice and inspiration that I intend for you to find here. Others require far deeper and more serious investigation. Only you can know the difference and act on it.

Be honest with yourself about what is really in your control, what needs sorting out with urgency and what can be helped by a book that is going to be referencing George Clooney multiple times. Give yourself a chance by being realistic. Do not try to be superhuman. Be judicious about what you're treating yourself for, why and how.

You do not need to prepare for a personality transplant

For some people it is transformative enough to hear the experiences of others and to know that other people also suffer with these same issues. They suddenly see: 'Oh, this is not me. It's a human thing. Why am I getting so hung up about it, as if it's only happening to me? It's happening to loads of people.' And their problem is solved, or at least minimized. But flipping that switch of awareness is not always that simple. I am constantly blown away by the depth of despair that many people are living with. Often it is couched as 'imposter syndrome' (especially by women, because this seems to have become a theme that women are encouraged to engage with). Younger people will often term it anxiety, especially social anxiety. Some of the challenges are practical and specific. ('I can only speak if there are slides. Don't take my slides away.') Others are nebulous and abstract but involve stasis and an inability to escape a comfort zone, no matter how uncomfortable reality has become. ('I just hate my life.') A lot of these messages come predominantly from women, I think because as women we are more encouraged to talk about these things. Women are accustomed to being expected to share. In fact, I think as a society we have an almost pathological need to insist that women talk about these insecurities, and a woman admitting to being self-assured and happy is seen as weird and 'a bit up herself'.

But I have also heard the same story, privately, from a lot of men. It can take longer to get to the heart of a problem with men as they admit confidence issues much less readily. But once they open up, the issues are identical: 'There are moments when I feel so undermined at work that I can barely function.' 'I think my immediate boss is bullying me but I can't be sure. A lot of their criticisms of me ring true.' 'How can I come across as authoritative without being arrogant?' 'Why do I keep being overlooked?' 'How can I speak like a leader without seeming too serious and boring?' 'How can I be more myself at work?' 'I can manage pretty much anything but I go to pieces in a meeting if a certain person is in the room.' 'I can start a speech but I go blank after three minutes' – or the opposite of this: 'I'm fine after I've been speaking for five minutes but I have no idea what I said to get through those first five minutes. It's a blur.' The knock-on effects are felt just as equally by men and women: problems with sleep, poor work–life balance, lack of support, no time for friendships outside work. And on it goes.

I have heard countless variations on these issues. They're often work-specific, but if you dig down they are replicated across many parts of our lives, including our personal relationships with our partners and children, and in the way that we plan our lives. I've often been asked to help someone tackle their public speaking or 'leadership projection' only to find that, actually, on a good day they're an excellent speaker but they just haven't had a good night's sleep for the best part of two years. Their problem is not so much their speaking or their leadership, it's just that they don't have very many good days. They don't need a public speaking coach – they need some camomile tea. In another instance, someone might want to work on the flow of a speech and on strengthening their presence but I can tell that something is distracting them. When it comes down to it, they're permanently worrying about their failings as a parent. This person also doesn't need a coach – they need to schedule regular activities with their child. Many things distract us and bring us down, and we're not always entirely aware of them or honest with ourselves about what they are. I know from my own experience that on stage I need to feel as prepared physic-ally as I am mentally: if I'm tired, dehydrated and feel like I look hideous (even if objectively I look fine), it doesn't matter how well-prepared I am or how great my material is, it's going to be an uphill battle. Whatever the issue, it all boils down to very simple wishes or desires. How can you feel ready to take on anything? How can you feel 'enough'? How can you step up when you are unprepared or under-prepared? How do you handle self-doubt? Do other people feel this insecure and what do they do about it?

What I have learned from thousands of interactions with readers, listeners and audiences at live events is that what people most want to know is: *How can I feel better about myself?* Finding your way to your own version of happy high status is the answer to all the questions above. This is not about a personality transplant or an enforced injection of extroversion or charisma. Nor do I want you to grow metaphorical jazz hands. More than anything else, the pages ahead are intended as a practical read to help you access your own personalized, unique version of effortless confidence.

How to get a piece of it

• Identify a time in your life when you felt at your best. This could be a memory from childhood, a birthday, a holiday, a moment in nature. Or it could be a time of professional pride, when you won an award or got a promotion or a pay rise, or received a meaningful word of praise. Whatever springs to mind is the right thing to investigate. (There's no right or wrong answer, just something that gives you good

feelings, no matter how mild those feelings –
though try to find something that gives you
intense good feelings. It's subjective. You are
looking to recall intensity of joy or pride.) Make
a note of that memory and give yourself some
time to think about how you felt, making notes
as you recall it. What feelings were you
experiencing? Where did you experience that
in your body? What expression did you have
on your face? What could you sense around
you? How did other people behave towards
you? Think about this moment as often as you
can over the next few days and try to notice if
you are ever experiencing the same feelings in
the present moment. In a later chapter, we will
explore how to summon happy high status into
your life more often. For now, just focus on
calling up the memory as often as you can.

- Know why you care about your confidence.
It's really important to identify as specifically
as you can why it is that you want to be
confident. Confidence is not the answer to
everything. And realistic confidence
incorporates vulnerability. This is not a means
of Teflon-coating yourself. There is no point in
becoming confident in the abstract because

you want to 'feel great every day' or 'never be hurt by anything'. Get specific and personal. What are you wanting to be confident *for*? What is the *aim* and how will confidence help you achieve this? What are the changes that would come about in your life if you were more confident? You need to know the answers to these questions in order to stay motivated and in order to appreciate the stakes involved. We only ever really change anything about ourselves when we understand the price of not changing. What do I mean by this? I mean that, for example, if you realize the cost of your low confidence is the inability to ask for a pay rise, then you can literally measure that cost financially. To know that number is motivating. (Usually depressing first. Then motivating.) Other costs could be: missed opportunities with family and friends because you're too preoccupied with your professional issues to enjoy life outside work; becoming physically ill with anxiety and stress; taking less pleasure in life because you're setting expectations ever lower . . . Ask yourself: what is the cost of my insecurity? What are the side effects? Is the cost worth it?

- Alongside the essential mental health disclaimer ('Do you actually need to talk to a professional?') is the importance of examining the context of your life. Frequently I've had conversations with people about their confidence and how they can better handle pressure or look more confident in the spotlight or in a leadership role. They will talk about it as if it's some kind of personal hang-up that is dominating their life and they will be full of blame and self-recrimination for their failings. Then after a few questions it will transpire that there are a lot of events in their life that are completely out of their immediate control or that require separate intervention – say, their company is going through a round of brutal redundancies, or they're recently bereaved, or they have recently had a health scare. The expression 'red flag' is overused but these kinds of situations are indeed red flags. There are moments when you need to give yourself time to get through a situation that is not of your making. And there are moments when it's worth working on your own state of mind. Don't confuse them. You cannot realistically work on your happy high status and hope to achieve results if you are in a major crisis situation. Face immediate challenges first. Sometimes it is necessary to work on resilience, or even simply survival, ahead of happy high status.

- What strengths do you have that you already use instead of confidence? Knowing your own strengths and leaning on them gives you a real feeling of inner calm. A lot of things can pull you through when your confidence fails: the ability to be well-prepared without being over-prepared; the ability to improvise or be spontaneous; the ability to ask the right questions at the right time. Know your strengths! If you are thinking, 'Well, I would do all these things if only I had the confidence . . .' then you are making excuses for yourself. You already have strengths. Dig deep, work out what they are and make sure you lean on them. Trusted friends and colleagues can be good at telling you what these are if you genuinely have no idea. (There is also a useful thing online called StrengthsFinder 2.0 if you like doing online quizzes that you have to pay for and you don't trust your friends or colleagues to tell you anything useful.)

Inspiration for vulnerable happy high status: inner calm

Traits: Softly spoken. Great listener. Supportive of others. Leads from the side or the back. Better at influencing than proclaiming. Prefers consensus to confrontation. Can accommodate a lot of competing ideas without feeling threatened. Light-hearted. Expressive. Contemplative. Carries lightness on the face.

Most useful for: People who feel that confidence is 'not for them' or 'something for annoying people'.

Who succeeds at this: **Brené Brown** – author and academic known for her research on shame and vulnerability, brilliant at expressing ideas calmly and clearly. **Isabel Allende** – writer and thinker who incorporates spirituality into her work. **Julia Samuel** – psychotherapist with a mellifluous voice, compassionate energy and enviable listening skills. **Karamo Brown** – *Queer Eye* TV-series presenter and activist who can equally hold attention and give others his full attention. **Pema Chödrön** – Buddhist nun who injects peaceful, meditative messages with humour and enthusiasm.

Chapter 2

BE LIKE A COMEDIAN (SORT OF)

WHERE STATUS COMES FROM AND HOW TO MASTER YOURS

Entertaining Happy High Status:
Playful Control

You have some kind of status whether you know it or not

Early on in my experience as a stand-up, I received a strange comment from an experienced comedy promoter I trusted and liked. After a gig, just over ten years ago, she said: 'You need to play higher status.' At the time I didn't really know what this meant. But it felt like important feedback. On that particular night I was secretly pleased about how the gig had gone because it had been 'all right' without being suspiciously too good. Early on when you're inexperienced you can have wildly successful gigs that are a complete fluke and lull you into complacency and a false sense of security. My aim at the time was to achieve consistent results. And in comedy that is incredibly difficult. You are always trying to push up the level of your performance so that the level of the 'worst' performances is always rising (because you can't have the best night every night). The ultimate goal is that your 'worst' is better than most people's best. That is the measure of professionalism in comedy.

This gig was at a nightclub where the room – a sticky

dance floor like something out of *Saturday Night Fever*, complete with random disco lights – was way too big for the audience and everyone was eating chicken-in-a-basket because it was part of the ticket deal. At that time I had got to the point where things like chicken-in-a-basket and sticky dance floors didn't put me off any more. I was learning to just do the job, even if the job was trying to engage people who were more focused on gnawing on poultry bones than anything else. I thought my cast-iron tolerance of the chicken-munching counted as confidence. It did, perhaps. But confidence is not quite the same as high status. And high status is not the same as happy high status.

My biggest worry back then was effortlessness: how to fake it? I was trying to improve my ability both to respond in the moment and to operate on stage in a way that felt natural and not forced. This is a very difficult part of stand-up comedy: you are usually working from a script but you have to make that script look and sound as if you just thought of it on the spot, as if it is most definitely not a script that you have memorized. Plus, you are 'acting' a version of yourself. But you need to give the illusion that you are not acting, you are being your authentic self. Get either of these two things wrong and the audience won't buy it. But don't make that look effortful, make it look natural. It's an incredibly contradictory process. How can that be 'authentic' and 'you' when it is an illusion and you are on a stage, delivering a pre-written monologue? How can any of that be effortless? No one cares about how difficult this is. You just have to get it right. While this is true of stand-up comedy, it's also true of any attempt to be 'effort-lessly confident' in any endeavour. It's the oxymoron from hell.

Happy high status is not (only) about coming across well on stage. It is *everything*.

It took me a long time to work out that 'status' – not confidence – is a big part of the answer to closing that gap between natural and unnatural, forced and effortless. And it took me even longer to understand that status is not just something that exists when you are up on stage on your own. In fact, we are constantly making unconscious calculations about status all the time, at every moment of our lives. Status profoundly affects how we view ourselves and how we are perceived by others. This quality of 'enter-tainer happy high status' – or 'charismatic happy high status' – is not about feeling like you have to amuse people all the time. It is about recognizing – as all entertainers do – that people are always watching you and drawing conclusions about you. You have status. You might as well play around with controlling it.

Life is full of petty humiliations, perceived slights and unimportant-but-wounding minor indignities, and we have to maintain our status in the face of them, to swallow our pride, to cushion our ego. Happy high status is about learning to rise above the shame and do what you were going to do anyway. Even if that means competing with fried chicken for attention. Over time, I realized that this was not simply a strategy for stand-up comedy: it is a strategy for anyone who needs to get people to listen, who wants to be able to stand their ground, recover from setbacks, take things in their stride. If you could feel like that the whole time, pretty much nothing would ever bother you. Goals.

It's essential to understand first, though, what it means when we are watching status on stage or on screen. When used in the context of performance and narrative, status is vital. It is relevant to a lot of branches of acting and performance, but is particularly important in the world of improv comedy (also known as impro or improvisation), a discipline that has a lot of crossover with stand-up because it frees up your creativity and helps with generating material. Because I was late to the comedy circuit – and older than most people on it by almost two decades – I wanted to make progress fast, stop messing up and experience as little failure as possible. Improv teaches you that defining your own status as a performer in relation to the audience is the key. They need to know at a glance what your status is.

What is meant by status 'in relation to the audience'? Every relationship is a status interaction. But the status interaction in stand-up is a really tricky one because obviously you are one person giving a monologue, ostensibly talking to yourself. It may not seem as if it's a 'relationship', but it is. Because even if we are standing alone in the spotlight and even if it seems as if it's one-sided, we are always standing in relation to others when we are talking to them. In everyday interactions, we don't often really need to ask the question: 'What vibe am I giving off? What's my status here?' Because most of the time we are simply 'being ourselves' and responding to situations without having to be self-conscious. We tend to accept subconsciously that some people will like our 'vibe' and some may not. Some may respect our status and some may not. That's life. We would drive ourselves mad if we worried about it all the time. And it's not necessary for us to do this anyway. But a comedian needs to know exactly what that 'vibe' or 'status' is and it needs to be consistent and unchanging. They need to communicate to an audience very quickly what their attitude is to the world. Where do they stand? Optimist or pessimist? Show-off or neurotic? Raconteur or misanthrope? Are they high status (examples of this could be posh, snobby, know-it-all or all three) or low status (coming across as slow-on-the-uptake, depressive, perpetually unlucky or all three)?

At first, this doesn't sound like a transferable dilemma. And there's no denying it: comedy monologues are a truly idiosyncratic art. But I've witnessed people stressing out about job interviews, generating social media content or preparing for a work presentation and having similar stresses. How do you look like you're meant to be doing that thing? How can you seem commanding without looking like a teacher? How can you be self-deprecating without doing yourself down? How can you communicate certainty and confidence fast? The same things you have to learn in comedy are the same things we get plagued by in real life. It's just on a different scale. These are all ways of saying: 'I don't know how to be the version of myself that this situation demands.' Or: 'I don't know what kind of status to play in this situation.'

If you think of a comedian or a comedy character you love, you will know immediately what their attitude is and you will immediately be aware of their status. Ricky Gervais's and Jimmy Carr's status is 'clever dick' (high status). Lucille Ball was ditzy (low status). Their clarity in communicating their character – which may or may not be based on their real self – is vital because they can't waste any time. If you are the comedian, with every second that the audience is trying to work out where you stand in relation to them and to the world, you are losing time to make them laugh and get them on your side. You have to collapse that moment of understanding as fast as you can.

If this sounds stressful, then it's only because in comedy it's a conscious task. In real life, we do this unconsciously all the time and it is second nature to us. To realize this is perhaps even more scary than trying to do it on purpose in comedy. We are constantly emitting clues and information about our status and how we stand in relation to each other. Because in real life we always stand in relation to someone else. In every dynamic in day-to-day life there is an unspoken, understood hierarchy: parent and child, boss and worker, teacher and student, stand-up and audience. All of our interactions are either respecting that dynamic and building on it or challenging it and pushing the boundaries. Even when we are alone, we have some kind of status or state of being that affects our frame of mind.

We are constantly communicating status to others

Long before I had heard of all these ideas, my only under-standing of 'status' used to be about social status: the drive for one-upmanship, keeping up with the Joneses and accu-mulating tons of superfluous possessions. (Alain de Botton explores this brilliantly in his book *Status Anxiety*.) This is a distraction. The theatrical way of thinking about status is different.

Status is explored in great depth in Keith Johnstone's seminal bible for performers, *Impro: Improvisation and the Theatre*, which came out in 1979. A director and play-wright, Johnstone was the first to identify and decode concepts that we know about instinctively as audience members when we are watching a drama or a comedy but that we rarely discuss or consciously process. These con-cepts really inform how we understand storytelling. We are constantly gauging who's up and who's down, who is the hero and who is the villain, which character 'ranks' higher than another, who has the upper hand in a relationship, whose status is in jeopardy. The very idea of drama itself is determined as much by plot (or perhaps even more so) as it is by the changing fortunes of the characters and how that affects their place in the social and emotional hierarchy.

This insight is important for performers because when we 'see' this evidence of status on stage or on screen (as opposed to imagining it when we read a book), we 'read' extra information about hierarchy through body language, facial expressions, tone of voice and, generally, non-verbal communication. In this context, status informs 'the emotional plot' of any relationship. Who's secretly in love? Who is lying? Who has a secret? Who is withholding information? Who can be trusted?

If you think of a sitcom like *Friends*, for example, the plot is fairly secondary and irrelevant, and you could watch the episodes in any order. The real plot of *Friends* is about the status of the characters in relation to one another and how that changes. A character's status might be defined by their station in life or by their class, or by how they're dressed or by their accent. But their status is also connected to their view of the world and how they express themselves.

Think of Chandler: he thinks he's high status but really he's low status because he's so petty. The comedy comes from the clash of those two things. Or Phoebe: she would also appear to be low status because she's scatty but we know that she is really high status because she is judgemental. In Johnstone's understanding, status might superficially be our station in life. Chandler is a data analyst (high status). Phoebe is a massage therapist (low status). But this is just the noun that describes us. More importantly, status – our 'real' status – is something that we do, the verb that describes how we move through life. It is the way that we act: with honesty or dishonesty; comfortable or uncomfortable with the hand we've been dealt; with meanness or with generosity; like a snob or like an empath. You can be a hopeless and wheedling queen (think of Queenie in *Blackadder*): high in social status but low in your opinion of yourself. Or you can be a supercilious handmaid (think of Offred in *The Handmaid's Tale*): supposed to be low status but refusing that designation.

Figuring out where your status sits

Johnstone explored this to help actors and improvisers define their characters on stage and be able to respond spontaneously and authentically to any development. It's particularly useful for improvisation, when you don't have a script and your character is not predefined either to yourself or to anyone else you're performing with. You can signal the direction of a scene by using status and giving other people around you something to respond to. You can decide your next move by thinking, 'What's the high status response here? And the low status response?' Example: a high status emotional response would be to play someone who is understanding and forgiving. A low status one would be to play the victim or to lash out. You can also signpost ideas and intentions to other improvisers by clearly signalling your emotional or social status. Without an understanding of status, how to signal it and how to watch out for it changing in others, you can't really hope to respond helpfully on stage if you are improvising and there's no script. It's a shorthand or a code that answers the question: 'How do I stand in relation to you and how might that affect what happens next?' When you learn how to portray and respond to status in improv, it becomes a game in which it's easy for others to see their potential next move.

When improvisers talk about 'status' in the context of a stage performance, they are talking about something deeper than the title on a business card or whether you are, say, a high-court judge or an escaped convict. Yes, of course, those are obvious types of status. But there could be a 'status battle' (an improv game) between two tramps. In fact there has to be this kind of battle on stage or on screen, otherwise the audience would get bored. Drama and fiction teach us that status is about so much more than money and the trappings of power. We see that you could be the richest and most successful person in the world and yet still have no status at home (because, for instance, your lover holds the power in that relationship as you love them more than they love you). These are the sorts of 'real power' and 'real status' clues that we are watching out for any time we are watching theatre, television or film. We have trained ourselves to look out for what's really going on and how that might help us work out what's going to happen next. Starting to observe status on stage and on screen, as well as in real life, is the first step to understanding where you want your own status to 'sit' and how you want it to be read by others.

If you are thinking, 'Wow, improv sounds great. Intense.

But great . . .', then you are right. It can be. It is entertaining to play around with your own status and realize how quickly it can switch, according to body language, tone of voice, posture. However, you might be thinking, 'I'm not sure about this improv stuff.' In which case, don't take it from me, take it from award-winning writer, actress and comedian Tina Fey, who has long extolled the benefits of using improv thinking in many areas of life. She describes it as 'a way to experience breaking out of the conventional, programmed ways we behave in most situations'. In other words: this is a way to play with and challenge our behaviour, and to understand that our status does not have to be fixed. We can dial it up and dial it down.

OK, I get what status is. But why do you have to say 'happy high status' all the time?

I first heard about extending the concept of status to 'happy high status' when I was taking part in an improv class with The Spontaneity Shop in north London (around the same time as the chicken-in-a-basket moment). Overnight it changed how I felt when I was on stage myself. I was taught by Alex MacLaren, an improviser and actor who is by anyone's standards an excellent example of a happy high status person. In class he used the term 'happy high status' to mean 'effortlessly charming' or 'your best dream cocktail-party self'. It means taking a high status version of yourself (you on a good-hair day, having just received a promotion or a proposal of marriage) and adding in a dose of 'happy' – unflappable, at ease, balanced. It's the kind of energy you might use on stage when you need to 'make friends' with the audience as the host. (The TV presenters Graham Norton and Lorraine Kelly are textbook happy high status.) But mostly, Alex explained, happy high status is not something that is useful on stage or during improvisation because it doesn't product conflict or drama of any kind. Which is precisely why it is useful in life.

In *The Improv Handbook: The Ultimate Guide to Improvising in Comedy, Theatre, and Beyond*, Alex's colleagues Tom Salinsky and Deborah Frances-White describe how students of improv comedy are often resistant to the idea that you can be 'likeable' but 'high status' at the same time. They first started using the expression 'happy high status' when they were developing an Edinburgh Fringe show that was like a dating game, involving audience participation. They needed people to behave on stage as if they were attractive and highly eligible: they told them to be 'happy high status'. It worked. (Alex explained: 'We suddenly found that we were all actually sexier.') This is a great example of playful control. We are used to thinking of 'high status' as meaning 'authority figure' or 'boss' and therefore unlikeable. But we believe happy high status when we see it manifesting as a combination of high status body language (still, calm, relaxed, unhurried) and smiling, charming behaviour (being kind and attentive to others, listening, making people laugh, feel at ease or feel welcome). When you witness this – and in an improv class you would experiment with it and attempt to demonstrate it – you finally understand that true status has nothing to do with your status in life. It's all about your behaviour, your self-perception and what you choose to display. The crucial part of this is that it's about what we *choose*. Once we know about how status works, we can use it on purpose. We are all always giving off signals and 'tells' to others that signify – consciously or unconsciously – how we expect them to treat us.

Why say 'happy high status' instead of just 'confidence'? And isn't this just another way of saying 'entitled'?

I want to underline the importance of approaching the question of confidence with fresh eyes. The expression 'happy high status' is appealing because it is unfamiliar. It is an uncomplicated way of loosely saying 'confidence' or 'charisma' but without any of the heavy connotations those kinds of words come with. From childhood we are very bound up in ideas of how we should behave, what others are thinking of us, what we are capable of, who and what we're 'allowed' to be, who is counted as a 'confident' person and who isn't. We are, essentially, confused between 'confident in a useful and productive way' and 'entitled in a damaging and controlling way'. This is why our reaction to high status characters can sometimes be negative: we resent their authority and think they can be full of themselves, and none of us wants to be like that.

For some people, the word 'confidence' on its own can traditionally feel intimidating and like a stretch too far. It can even feel dangerous. In the past, many population groups, including women, have been ostracized, shamed or punished for being 'too confident', for asking for too much, for stepping out of line. Confidence is frequently – mistakenly – used as a synonym for entitlement. So woe betide you if you act confident and others think you are entitled to certain things, if you are not in the right social grouping.

No wonder there's a wariness. Alongside this hesitation, there can also be a misplaced certainty about what confidence is. It's confusing and contradictory. We both revere and despise confidence. We revere it because it holds a mystery, a mystique. It can never be quite proven or unproven. It can be undone in a second. It can be very real and yet suddenly prove to be unjustified. Think, for example, of a sportsperson or a team who are genuinely confident of success, and yet still they fail. Or of a person whose confidence comes from a sense of entitlement – because of their social position – and yet who behaves in a way that, instead of inspiring confidence in others, makes people scorn them. We despise confidence because sometimes people carry it and benefit from it whom we deem undeserving. And we envy it because some people use it to do things we wish we could do.

Both of these extremes – the reverence and the suspicion of confidence – reinforce contradictory ideas we have heard since childhood: 'Just believe in yourself and magic will happen' and its twin opposite, 'What have you got to be so cocky about? Wipe that smile off your face.' This is incredibly confusing, especially because, as I've mentioned, confidence cannot be objectively measured or quantified in the same way as strength, athleticism or intelligence. So there's a temptation to give up on the whole idea of confidence, especially if it feels like an effort. Why bother believing in yourself at all if it's so fragile and unquantifiable? After all, it's impossible to know where the line is before you're deemed *too* confident and accused of 'getting too big for your boots'. Nobody wants people to think they are smug or arrogant, even if we all know deep down that accusations of overconfidence are often wielded by others simply to keep us in our place. Indeed, this kind of name-calling or 'confidence-shaming' is usually really about conformity and control. All the same, you have to be brave or foolish to risk being branded as conceited. (And I write as someone whose surname literally means 'bighead'.) It is easier to denigrate the confidence of others and denounce the whole game as fake than it is to foster a real sense of your own confidence, independent of the evaluations of others.

When these ideas are so weighted down with baggage, it helps to have an expression that speaks for itself but that hasn't been rammed down your throat since childhood. ('Why can't you just be more confident?' 'What makes him so confident?' 'What has she got to be so confident about?' 'Some people have too much confidence . . .') I found that the more I channelled happy high status in what I was doing, the more I could let go of these precon-ceptions and the more easily I moved through life and had genuine, unforced self-assurance. I shook off failures and 'stage deaths' quicker. I didn't dwell self-indulgently when things went well. I'm not sure I became 'sexier' but maybe that's master-level stuff. Or maybe I was already just incredibly sexy. Only joking. Especially if my children are reading this.

But I did find that the practice of forcing myself to be happy high status on stage, to be 'entertaining', to exert that playful control, was transformative. It's a muscle that I started to exercise. It became a state of being that I wanted to be in more often. As happy high status increas-ingly became something that I could recognize and pinpoint in myself and in others, I began to think: *What if you didn't use that just for on stage? What if you used it all the time in life?* Over time I began to wonder in a weird utopian way about what it would mean if everyone did it. *What kind of world would we be living in if everyone was happy high status all the time? If everyone focused on being their most amenable, most generous, least petty self?* I'm not pretending for a second that I have mastered this in day-to-day life, on stage or really anywhere. But sometimes asking the right questions is enough of a place to start. There's a saying in therapy: 'Awareness is curative.' Once you are aware of the existence of happy high status, you start to see it everywhere.

How to get a piece of it

- Dig deeper into those moments and 'good
  memories' you identified where you were
  happy high status. Highlight them. Make a
  habit of revisiting them. The trick to being
  happy high status – relaxed, unchallenged, not
  seeking to dominate or be dominated – is to
  learn and almost memorize what you are like
  when you are in that frame of mind
  unconsciously and then replicate it consciously.
  This is not beyond anyone's capability: very
  few people in good physical health are
  miserable low status all the time. We can all
  find a moment or a memory when our status
  was heightened. The more you can think of
  those moments – of triumph, pride, celebration,
  achievement, calm, joy – the more you can
  analyse how you felt in that moment, what
  your body language was like, where your
  mind went to at that particular time. If you can
  discipline yourself to think about this, make
  notes and remember it on a regular basis, then
  you will start to think about how you can 'trick
  yourself' into that state even when nothing has
  happened to make you feel it.

- Find adjectives that feel less stressful than 'confident' to describe how you need to be. In some instances we need to be open, warm, fluid, articulate, welcoming, unintimidating, vulnerable, supportive. In other instances we need to be comprehensive, concise, clear, unflappable, knowledgeable . . . Make your job easier by being precise about the definition of what is required. It sounds weird but taking away the word 'confident' and replacing it with another word that will do the same job but feels more comfortable to you – that can sometimes be enough to make you more confident.

- Reframe the goal. If people are preparing for a talk, for example, they can become fixated on projecting confidence even when their task is to deliver information that is incredibly boring, though important. Or it might even be boring and *unimportant*. (Hey, we all have to earn a living. No judgement. Often we are required to be confident in situations that are not entirely of our choosing.) Clarity, urgency, efficiency and realism are, in fact, just as useful to you as confidence in that situation. Pinpoint the qualities you really need, especially if they are things that are easy and quick to work on. Clarity, for example, is easy to work on: don't make more than three points, keep your language simple, pause between points. This is far more realistic and actionable than something as grandiose and vague as 'becoming more confident'. Plus, clarity will have the side effect of actually making you look more confident anyway. Remember: confidence is sometimes an irrelevant factor. Are you certain that 'confidence' is the thing you need to work on? Can this thing be done without confidence?

Inspiration for entertaining happy high status: playful control

Traits: Fits the traditional definition of charismatic or extrovert. Comfortable in the spotlight. Happy to volunteer to lead. Enjoys being listened to but also capable of giving space to others when it's their turn. Happy to take risks. Doesn't take themselves seriously.

Most useful for: People who might be inclined to be high status without being happy high status and who want to know how to command attention without sucking all the oxygen out of the room. People who have been told they are 'too much'.

Who succeeds at this: **Tig Notaro** – comedian with slow-talking, gentle energy who uses suspense and charm to control the room. **Gina Yashere** – explosive comedian who knows just when to dominate and just when to rein it in. **Michelle Wolf** – stand-up who uses consummate charm to subvert expectations with 'iron fist in velvet glove' energy. **Trevor Noah** – comedian and presenter with suave and commanding energy but who knows how to be hard-hitting when he needs to. **Julia Roberts** – Oscar-winning actress with effortless charm and self-effacing wit who never pushes into smugness.

Chapter 3

BE LIKE A WISEGUY

MAFIA ENERGY WITHOUT THE MURDERING

Dominant Happy High Status:
Charismatic But Deadly

'He handled the situation with quiet authority and a real elegance.'

When Ray Liotta died in May 2022, *Goodfellas* director Martin Scorsese remembered the moment that first persuaded him to cast the actor. The assessment stands out because it encapsulates a particular kind of happy high status, maybe one with a bit of edge, especially in the context of mafia movies. Scorsese is unwittingly describing dominant happy high status here: an irresistible charisma ('quiet authority') with a hint of coldness ('real elegance'). Scorsese and Liotta first met when Liotta was auditioning for the role of Henry Hill, the mafia associate at the heart of *Goodfellas*. At the time, Liotta himself considered that he was not a frontrunner for the role because he was not a big Hollywood name. Nonetheless, thanks to the moment where he displayed this combination of authority and elegance, he was cast. *Goodfellas* went on to become one of the best movies about the mafia of all time, gaining six Oscar nominations, including a win for Best Supporting Actor for Joe Pesci. (Interestingly, Ray Liotta was not himself nominated for any of *Goodfellas*' multiple award mentions. I have a fangirl theory about this: his portrayal of Henry Hill feels so real and so successfully happy high status – despite the character being a mass murderer – that it's like he's in a documentary and it's everyone else around him who is acting.)

So how can a mafia killer be happy high status? And what are we supposed to learn from this? A character who keeps a handy spade in the back of the car in order to bury his victims doesn't sound like the most inspiring example of aspirational humanity. But there's so much to learn from this role model about the intentional and selective borrowing of the attitudes and traits of confidence. The movie is about the rise and fall of Liotta's character, who does all the 'right' (i.e. wrong) things in life in order to become one of the mafia's top 'wiseguys' but ends up paranoid, delusional and drug-addicted. It's a movie about the mafia and what we now call 'toxic masculinity'. But it's also a movie about how far a certain kind of confidence can take you.

Henry Hill is a sociopath from the start. But he has his charms (yes, authority and elegance) – he just channels them in the wrong direction. From the beginning, Scorsese's (or, possibly, Liotta's) intention for this charac-ter was that audiences would empathize with him and be able to see how he had gone from being one sort of person – genuine happy high status – to another sort of person – warped happy high status. The distinction is relevant because this kind of dominant happy high status – which is incredibly powerful, persuasive, seductive – can easily morph into something unpleasant or even psycho-pathic. I think many people avoid being charming, taking the lead, asserting dominance, because they fear this escalation. But in real life that kind of charisma, with the deadly removed, is a trait that can actually be used to soothe and reassure.

After Ray Liotta's death, Scorsese recalled the moment he first glimpsed that quality in the actor. Liotta was crossing a hotel lobby to speak to Scorsese when the actor was stopped en route by a wall of security guards. Scorsese remarked: 'Instead of throwing a fit and demanding that he be allowed through, he reacted quietly and calmly, observed the rules and patiently defused the situation. He looked at me, I looked at him, and we signalled that we would talk, and he walked away. I watched it all very closely, and *I saw him handle the situation with quiet authority and a real elegance.*' This is a perfect description of dominant happy high status. The director knew in witnessing that moment that Liotta would be able to carry off the part of a man who looks as if he would fit in with the mafia – but who also has the genuine lack of ego, ordinariness and low-key charm that would make the audience sympathize with him. The plot just added the 'deadly' part.

Mafia movies are fascinating to watch for this quality. Although the male roles are usually more prominent, for obvious reasons, you can observe it in the female characters, too. You know these characters are going to end up being bad people. But we have to find something about them that is charismatic, understandable, attractive.

Because who wants to watch a movie about people who are horrible from beginning to end? It's worth examining why we are drawn to these characteristics, even when they are worn by people whose aims are at best selfish and narcissistic and at worst criminal and murderous. How powerful would it be if these characteristics were harnessed and identified, and used for another purpose?

Borrowing benign behaviour from bad people

What has this *Goodfellas* example got to do with our confidence if we are not planning to transport a corpse in the boot of our car? Well, a lot. We take for granted the abundance of role models and influential types to identify with in books. As the novelist Iris Murdoch phrased it: 'One constantly takes prototypes from literature who may actually influence one's conduct.' Well, this is the same principle, but for TV-binge-watching instead of reading. This is what I mean by 'intentional and selective borrowing'. We're not talking about copying someone else's behaviour wholesale, because none of us can become another person. The point is to be judicious in our observation of dominance and in how we choose to transfer it on to ourselves. A character like Henry Hill presents an illustration of the body language, human interactions and social ease that can be borrowed for good not evil. And we are surrounded by these useful character examples on screen. No one is going to sign up to the '*Goodfellas*

Self-Help Guide to Great Communication (Comes With Free Revolver)', but what if we all behaved like we were in the mafia but never committed any crimes? What if we can borrow the hallmarks of confidence and authority from anyone and adapt them for our own use? I know women will be reading this and thinking, 'Ray Liotta in *Goodfellas* is not really my role model.' But why not? If you can take 1 per cent of that energy and use it to get a pay rise, to be heard in a negotiation, to say yes to something you would usually say no to, and to get your twelve-year-old to load the dishwasher (sorry, that's just me), then why not?

This extreme example of someone whose behaviour no one would seriously want to emulate shows that we can 'borrow' from anywhere and it doesn't mean we're copying or 'trying to be like a man'. (Or, for men, trying to be like an alpha or a sports jock. Or, for anyone: trying to be someone that we're not.) This is in contrast to advice that was commonly given in the 1980s and the 1990s. Some of the most striking moments during interviews on my podcast *How to Own the Room* have come when women – always over the age of fifty – have talked about moments in their early careers thirty or forty years ago when it was generally accepted that 'behaving more like a man' was the right way to 'get ahead'. Several women I've interviewed have recounted how, in boardroom situations, they would adopt stereotypically superficial male behaviours in order to be taken seriously. Aline Santos, Chief Brand Officer at Unilever, remembered wearing a men's jacket in her first board meeting. She would also wear aftershave instead of fragrance because she thought a feminine scent would be distracting. And she wore glasses – even though she didn't need them – in order to look 'intellectual'. While I admire the women who did the difficult and irritating work that they had to do in order to fit into those rooms, times have moved on. That kind of cultural 'borrowing' is no longer necessary. Younger women recount completely different experiences: standing their ground on dress codes so that they don't have to pretend to be something they're not, wearing trainers to work as a point of principle, refusing to conform to some superficial 'ideal'. (The more old-school perceptions, by the way, are not confined to women: I've had men ask me if they should wear glasses for a speech to 'have more gravitas'.)

These standards go beyond gender stereotypes. I was speaking at an event for 'women in leadership' recently and a young woman came up to me afterwards who said, 'Thank you for not being a size eight.' (I am not a skinny person.) It took me a moment to understand her point but I suddenly realized exactly what she meant. There is a stereotypical image of what a 'woman in leadership' should look like: tall, slim, power-suited, wearing heels and with a mane of swishy blow-dried hair. This stereotype excludes many – most? – women from leadership by default. None of us should be seeking to 'be like' or 'look like' anyone else. We should be seeking to shape the world in a way that feels right to us. There is an unspoken idea that still persists: 'If I look a certain way and do certain things, and conform to a certain expectation, then certain rewards will come to me.' Even if it were true and it actually worked – and I don't think that's the case any more, if it ever was – then that is a miserable way to live: 'As long as I pretend to be someone else, I can get what I want.' It's not a great trade-off, is it?

This extreme mafia example, then, is designed to show that we can afford to broaden out our influences, to assert our dominance. Actors do this all the time when they're creating a character. They will borrow a turn of phrase or a facial expression from someone in their childhood, they will base their physicality on someone they saw in passing or they will enter a space in the way that their uncle used to walk into the room. These are influences, flavours and inspirations that no one else could guess and that no one else needs to know about but that help them form that character. They don't try to 'be like' that person or do an impression of them. They borrow traits and take them on and off just as you would clothes from a wardrobe. People often say 'I'm channelling my inner Madonna' or 'Chris Hemsworth is my spirit animal.' (Insert your alpha choice of Hollywood actor or showbiz diva here.) We jokingly say these things as a way of indicating that we're looking for an injection of courage or energy. But what if we interpreted this a little more literally and really did try to channel dominant happy high status traits, intentionally?

Anti-heroes with their badness removed are useful. Iris Murdoch again: 'Plato remarks in *The Republic* that bad characters are volatile and interesting, whereas good characters are dull and always the same.' We struggle to 'be like' perfect or ideal characters whether real or fictional, as we find them either uninteresting or so perfect that they're intimidating. How could we possibly live up to them? A 'bad' character gives us something to steal from and improve upon. Yes, in the mafia films, the behaviour of characters like Henry Hill is duplicitous and transactional: these men are charming because they are sociopaths and want to control others. But *Goodfellas* is a great film because it shows – without moral judgement – that these behaviours are effective. They get results. What if we use them not to create an international crime syndicate but in order to foster goodwill and cooperation?

Binge-watch your way to happy high status

When you start to look around for examples of happy high status behaviour to emulate and model, you rapidly find that you're spoiled for choice. The trick is to be open-minded enough – as actors have to be – to see that great characters are not one-dimensional. You might not want to be like Logan Roy from *Succession* (actor Brian Cox) as he's a cantankerous, cold-blooded, ruthless gazillionaire who would betray his own children for a better business deal. But you can watch his command of a room and how he dominates and directs a conversation, and you can squirrel away that body language for your own purposes. He adopts intense stillness and a sparing use of gestures, selective strong eye contact (some people are worthy of his gaze, others are not) and short, direct sentences – he never rambles. Supposing you are a mild-mannered people-pleaser who finds that you are overlooked and rarely listened to. If you were to adopt just a handful of these mannerisms, you might find that over time people responded to you differently. You would certainly feel more control and agency over your own habits – and a lot of our struggle with confidence, especially when we're speaking in front of others, is governed by the fact that we've got into bad habits that reveal our lack of confidence and reinforce it by lowering our status. These things include fidgeting, flinching, shifting posture from side to side, overuse of hands, raised shoulders and shrugging generally – gestures that make us look hunched instead of taking up space . . . I could go on. You won't see Logan Roy (or any mafia bosses) doing these things. Unless they're having a bad day and are about to get whacked.

We can learn a lot about extremes of power by looking at these characters. Also, it's a great excuse for binge-watching. ('Yes, boss, I am working from home today. What project am I working on? Oh, I'm honing my leadership skills by analysing how Paul Giamatti interacts with a dominatrix on *Billions*.') If you watch with the sound off, you can study the body language of (usually) men of preposterously high status displaying one-upmanship. *Goodfellas* works brilliantly for this. Or *The Godfather*, *Casino*, *Mad Men*, *The Sopranos* . . . You don't need dialogue to tell who is boss, who is the listener, who is the watcher, who is the threat. You can see and feel it. And these highly stylized displays don't just happen in films where someone is likely to leave a dead horse's head on an acquaintance's pillow. They also happen in real life in marketing meetings that have overrun.

We are not used to seeing as many examples of this kind of equivalent behaviour in women but that is now changing. And there are some amazing displays of dominant happy high status (of both the genuine and warped kinds) in the female characters in shows like *Succession*, *Ozark*, *The Handmaid's Tale*, *House of Cards* and *Borgen*. Elsewhere, female characters with maximum menacing high status are often complicated lone wolves in fantastical universes: Carice van Houten as Melisandre in *Game of Thrones*, Angelina Jolie as Maleficent, Kathryn Hahn as Agatha in *WandaVision*. All three of these are basically variations on the vengeful, immortal, time-travelling witch who wants to control a kingdom and/or time itself. So, yes, fantastical and not seemingly possessing transferable real-life skills . . . But their projection of status is fascinating and motivating. Even if you are not using it to wipe out entire populations.

Increasingly we're seeing these complicated high status roles occupied by as many women as men in contemporary movies and on television. The principle of 'you have to see it to be it' applies heavily here: if we see more women (and people from all different backgrounds) in dominant happy high status roles in on-screen drama, there is a normalizing effect. How else do we know what it looks like when a president enters a room and that president is a woman? All the same, I think it pays to take inspiration wherever you can find it, whether it's sci-fi (Sean Young as Rachael in *Blade Runner*, a persuasive and powerful advanced android who believes she is human) or a cartoon (Penelope Pitstop in *Wacky Races*, the most glamorous and chill racer on the track). It might appear to be more straightforward to draw from real-life 'office' or 'work' examples, but, to be fair, if you're facing a job interview, you might get better results channelling Cate Blanchett as Hela in *Thor: Ragnarok* (goddess of death and single-handed massacrer of armies) rather than the more 'realistic' Julia Louis-Dreyfus as *Veep*'s Selina Meyer (the fictional first US woman president). Hela rebuilds the army of the undead. Selina is the most gloriously ineffective politician in world history. Could you have any stronger 'goals' energy? Why not be inspired by women who don't like doing things by halves?

It's interesting that actresses are often interrogated at length about how on earth they managed to make a dominant happy high status character entirely believable. With women, it's frequently assumed that the behaviour on show is so unusual that the actress must only be able to behave like that because *she is actually like that in real life*. When Robert De Niro plays a mobster, no one asks if he is secretly a mobster himself. It's almost as if it's easier for audiences to believe that a man can take a high status mantle on and off, no problem, because male high status behaviour is familiar and ubiquitous. Sharon Stone has talked often about the problems she had after portraying a preposterously dominant happy high status character (the warped version), *Basic Instinct*'s Catherine Tramell, the ice-pick-wielding bestselling thriller writer whose plots bear a remarkable resemblance to real-life killings. This character was so uncanny and so unusual – a psychopathic, self-possessed woman – that Stone was unable to shake her off. Stone was typecast after playing this role, and ridiculed and humiliated for being 'overly sexual'. In an award acceptance speech in 2019, Stone referred to the moment in *Basic Instinct* when she was asked to cross and uncross her legs while wearing no underwear: 'Thank you for choosing me as Woman of the Year because there was a time when all I was, was a joke.' It is not until thirty years later that she has been able to underline the message that she was playing a role: Catherine Tramell is not her. Catherine Tramell is – obviously – simply a high status persona that Sharon was able to adopt for the duration of that filming. It's scary that anyone would think otherwise.

One thing everyone needs to know about (most) actors is that they do not choose roles because they think their personality is close to the character they play, or because it will be easy for them. They choose that role because it will be hard. Why does this matter to the rest of us? Because it shows that transformation is possible – and that creativity and imagination can alter our behaviour in all kinds of useful ways. But it also shows that it requires intention. One of the most striking recent examples of a high

status – and sometimes happy high status – female character is Shiv Roy in *Succession*, played by Sarah Snook. Shiv
is a complicated, difficult character poised between comedy and tragedy. She is the only daughter in a group of
heirs vying for the attention of their tycoon father. Snook
has to play the role in such a way that we take Shiv seriously and don't just laugh at how ridiculous she is (even
though there are moments when she is plainly ridiculous).
She has to make Shiv seem menacing at times and worthy
of admiration at others. She has to project vulnerability,
idiocy and power all at once. Snook initially turned down
the role, believing that as a relative unknown from Aus-
tralia she was being invited to try for it just so that her
name would attract bigger, American names to the role.
(This recalls Ray Liotta's reaction to his *Goodfellas* cast-
ing.) Her refusal eventually meant that she was offered
more money to accept the role. And her initial lack of self-
assurance was also crucial in helping her to form the
character. Although *Succession* is heavily scripted, in some
scenes actors are encouraged to improvise and change
lines. In the first series Snook was working out the correct
accent for Shiv and didn't feel completely comfortable in
the character. So instead of improvising in the 'wrong'
accent, she made the choice to have Shiv sit back and look
as if she is sitting on an unvoiced opinion in some scenes.
This ended up being a whole new direction for the character. When we are watching her, we know that Shiv gets her
status from the fact that she has a strong opinion but will
pick her moment to voice it. Plus, say what you like about

Shiv, I would argue that these kinds of decisions make Sarah Snook exceedingly dominant happy high status. Sometimes less is more. And truly comfortable status is often more easily projected by silence, patience or a neutral choice.

Transferring this safely and legally to real life

To reiterate: one of the reasons that status matters so much in narrative drama – especially narrative drama where people are committing criminal acts – is because it's so *engrossing*. Without this kind of status play, the stakes are lowered so far as to become non-existent and then we just don't care about the outcome of a story. In fiction, no one is truly neutral because they would be too boring to maintain our interest. In real life, it would help our sanity and our happy high status to be close to neutral or *just boring enough*. Unfortunately, in real life we struggle to maintain genuine neutrality because status and power play get in the way. Whether it's ongoing sibling drama, hang-ups from the family chaos we lived through as children, colleagues who rub us up the wrong way, someone cutting us up in traffic, a perceived insult on social media or a genuine example of mean, wounding behaviour on- or offline, most of us are often on our guard. It's worth thinking about whether all this drama is really necessary. In a fictional narrative – whether it's TV, film or a novel – drama is more than necessary: the story will not work without it.

But in real life? A situation is likely to play out a lot more successfully – and less painfully – without the drama. What happens if you remove the status battle? What happens if you walk away from a power play? What difference does it make if you lower the stakes? What if you remove ego and personal slights from the picture? In fiction and on screen, the temperature is always being turned up to force an outcome. In real life, happy high status is achieved by turning the temperature down.

When you are writing or performing drama, you are constantly looking for ways of upping the stakes and making the motivations of the characters explicit. This character, for example, always fights back because when they were a child it was the only way they got attention. This other character always backs down – but hates themselves for it. We 'buy' these backstories in fiction because we recognize the truth of these situations and we can see how easily a character could get trapped inside those ideas. It would not be interesting if the character suddenly said, 'Oh, actually I'm not going to respond that way any more because I've realized that I'm just getting my emotional buttons pushed.' Or if they did do this, that would be the end of the narrative. In real life, however, we can decide to call ourselves out on these things any day of the week. We can choose not to react. We can choose to behave differently. We can choose to seek a second opinion or an outside view. We can choose to question our 'natural' reaction. We can choose the 'boring' reaction. We can choose to put on the mantle of high status and mould it however we want.

I wish more people knew about this because it does not require a huge shift. And it is really not that difficult. It is about sizing up a situation and making a sober judgement in answer to the questions: 'What is really needed here? What if I chose not to overreact? What does an under-reaction look like?' Sarah Snook's real-life, human reaction to feeling uncertain about her on-screen character was wise: buy yourself time by stepping back. It had the unintended genius consequence of giving the character of Shiv *more* status, not less. It required Snook to take a leap of faith and not do the thing that she *thought was expected* (i.e. to contribute and improvise lines). It was actually a more advanced, bold form of improvisation: 'What happens if I do nothing?' Happy high status sometimes comes from stepping back, assessing, doing less, waiting. This is the opposite of over-delivering, of being overtly conscientious, of burying yourself in 'busywork' to show that you're 'working really hard'. Often we retreat into these behaviours at work because our emotional buttons have been pushed. We fear being accused of underperforming so we dig in harder. We are angry at being overlooked so we overproduce. We are desperate for approval so we go into 'performance' mode.

Leadership and status work best when they are worn lightly. When there is ease, patience and the 'chill' that comes with lowering the stakes. These qualities create space: for a surprising discovery, for something that couldn't be planned, for the solution no one else thought of. This is the safe, healthy version of dominant happy high status: having the guts to pave the way for something. This way of thinking is common in art, performance and creativity. But it is not something we talk about much as a work skill and it is certainly not a trait anyone is consciously encouraged to acquire, especially not women who have had it drummed into them that the way to succeed is to work exceptionally hard and be brilliant at everything you do – or else you will be criticized and punished. Hard work has its place but it does not guarantee status. I was talking to a male CEO the other day about why certain industries have a problem with recruiting and retaining women at senior levels. He said, 'The ones who don't make it in my industry – and it's mostly women I'm talking about – are the ones who are always trying to do the right thing or ace the test as if they are still at school and their work is going to be marked. It works when you are junior. You can be diligent and hard-working and thorough and you will go far. The older you get and the higher up you go, though, none of that is relevant.' I said, 'You mean, they need to learn how to bullshit?' He looked at me sharply: 'No, I don't. The men who are like that are bad enough. We don't need more people like that.' He thought about it for a moment: 'I'm just talking about people who can think on their feet.'

This is the lesson to take from these displays of dominant happy high status: read the situation and be ready to react. Don't assume there is a set path. Be ready to make it up as you go along, but not by 'bullshitting', by relying on your instincts, knowledge and experience. I was reminded of what Scorsese saw in Liotta in that hotel: the ability to improvise, to back down without losing face, to be graceful, to make it up as you go along and to go with the flow. If you can be seen doing that – and not with criminal intent – it's impressive. Like a non-mafia, legitimate, considered definition of the expression 'ducking and diving'. What does it look like when you try to do that a little more?

'But, Viv, I am not an actor.'

I know. I hear you. I promise you are not being asked to 'act'. You are not even being asked to 'act as if'. I am not asking you to join the mafia, either. I am simply asking you to observe and question how status is portrayed and to think about how that plays out in your own life. It may not be comfortable to examine how we react or how we come across. We may be afraid of being fake or of coming across as something we're not. We may want to retreat into the defence that happy high status behaviours are only for celebrities or actors, or 'charismatic people' or 'show-offs who were born that way'. But the myth that 'some things just come naturally to some people' is just a way of keeping us in our place. It's an attractive myth, of course, because it gives us a built-in excuse: 'I just wasn't born to do this.' 'I guess I don't have funny bones.' 'I've been shy since I was a child.' 'I can't copy Ray Liotta or Sharon Stone.' 'I can't command a room.' 'No one would believe me as a mafia boss anyway. Leave it to De Niro.' It lowers expectations – our own and those of others. If you're thinking this way, it's just because you are scared of dominant happy high status.

Standing by this myth allows us to imagine a world where people fit neatly into boxes: those who can (because they were born that way) and those who can't (because it just wasn't meant to be). It allows us to venerate 'greatness' (power, status, leadership, artistic achievement) without overthinking it. Because often the things that we celebrate as 'greatness' are hard to understand and define: beautiful artworks that seemed pointless when they were being made and yet reveal something important long after their creation; mathematical and scientific discoveries that remain frustratingly out of reach for years until the day of the breakthrough; the brio and grace of an effortless performance of dance, speaking or music; a leader who appears just at the right moment . . . There is seemingly an element of mystery to all these things, and that mystery is both deepened and easily, comfortingly explained if we can say, 'Clearly, that was just meant to be. It can't be reverse-engineered by the likes of me.' This myth is a sad one but it defines many people's lives: 'It doesn't come naturally to me so there's no point.'

But even though it's long since been debunked by academics, psychologists and coaches, this myth of 'natural talent' or 'natural dominance' is not an easy one to abandon. Every language has powerful words to describe the magical qualities of people who seem to be able to glide through life, convincing others of whatever they want. You could call it 'chutzpah'. It has always struck me that a lot of these qualities stem from family interactions and how we deal with children. These ideas and turns of phrase are common in families to explain why one sibling is different from another, why one relative is favoured over another, why one person seems better at something than another. They are basically a form of family shorthand or almost a sort of gossip. They are part of the sweet and well-meaning but essentially useless things that we say about babies: 'Oh, look at him kick, he's going to be a footballer.' (No, it is just a human being who is learning how to use their legs.) 'With those fingers, she could be a pianist.' (No, it is just a baby chewing its hands.) There's something contradictory about this chat: on the one hand, we tell babies (not that the babies are listening or can understand) that they are going to be world-class athletes and performers. On the other hand, as soon as they get old enough to actually train to do any of these things, we usually tell them that those things are reserved only for those who are 'naturally gifted'. I think we are often scared of real achievement, real confidence, of the guts and hope and leap of faith that it takes to try to make a difference in the world. So we lie about it: we lie when we say that being able to walk means you will win the Olympics and we lie when we say that certain things are reserved only for certain people. The truth lies somewhere in the middle, between the application of hard work and the leap of faith of improvisation. Happy high status of any variation lies in knowing the difference: sometimes you need to put the hours in and sometimes you need to think on your feet.

This is the lesson we learn from actors and their fictional creations. We are not limited in our range of behaviours. We do not need to be held back by our own definitions of who we are. We are able to come across in more ways than we can imagine. The trick for all of us in adulthood is to examine our perceived limitations and to begin to question them. Is it really true that you are 'not a confident person'? Or are you just a perfectly normal, ordinary human being who occasionally has moments of low confidence? There's a world of difference between those two definitions. The first ('I'm not a confident person') allows you to say no, to turn down opportunities, to hide. Because you've given yourself a reason. The second ('I have moments when I'm not confident') allows you to experiment, take risks, have a go. Because you are not trapped in a permanent definition.

This is what actors do when they create a character: they take a flavour, a feeling, an experience, and they expand it in order to create another version of themselves. Including, if necessary, the part of a psychotic witch who wants to set fire to the galaxy. (I can feel the spirit of Hela possessing me again . . .) But this does not have to be far-fetched or for thespians only. It's a life skill. If you can admit to yourself that there are circumstances – however rare – when you feel good, when you feel confident, when you are happy high status, maybe even when you are a little bit *dominant happy high status*, then you can carry those feelings into other moments. An actor might carry them into a scene or into a character. You can move them across into different parts of your life. Can you take some of those feelings – the ones from when you feel good – and 'overlay' them on to bad circumstances? Once you start thinking of yourself as a laboratory experiment (and one where surprising changes can emerge), then you start to see things differently. You start to see evidence and patterns. You start to see that you are not one thing, that you are not limited, that you have options.

Our attitude towards the malleability and flexibility of our confidence is vital: we need to believe that we are capable of operating in a slightly different way. In terms of confidence, it really means having to let go of the idea that some people are just naturally self-assured or naturally better at 'acting as if'. Which is not to pretend for a second that anyone can be an Academy Award-winning actor just by believing in themselves: that is skilled work that requires rigorous discipline *and* self-belief. But we are not aiming to win an Oscar: we are just aiming to borrow traits, find inspiration and switch up our behaviour very slightly. And that is more than achievable.

How to get a piece of it

- Now that this idea has lodged in your mind, you will probably find yourself watching characters on screen and thinking, 'Is that happy high status?' You might even ask yourself what kind of variation it is: dominant, vulnerable, entertaining? There's no right or wrong answer to this, it's just a way of finding out what you are impressed by, what you are not impressed by, analysing how those results are achieved and allowing that to seep into you as if by osmosis. You will soon start to identify behaviours that are 'too dominant' for you or 'too entertaining'. Think about what you can learn from that. Do you want to avoid that kind of self-assurance completely? Or could you take a flavour of it? Be especially aware of the kind of behaviour we don't see much in 'real life'. The portrayals of the dominant happy high status women in *Ozark*, *Succession* and *House of Cards*, in particular, are unusual because we see women operating in circumstances that are not readily observable. (By which I mean that we have seen plenty of portrayals of men in extreme leadership roles – whether as company bosses or mafia bosses. We don't readily see as many examples of this behaviour in women.)

- Be direct and concise. Choose your words. Don't ramble. Remember Logan Roy in *Succession*: the status comes from stillness of the body and an economy of words. Watch any movie or TV show that portrays power in any way and you will often spot, alongside the still, self-possessed high status types, the low status character who jiggles about and rambles and gives too much information and keeps talking when they should shut up . . . and you will feel in your gut that they are not long for this world. We all know that this habit lessens our status, makes us harder to listen to and, er, makes us more likely to be killed off. How to stop it? Listen to yourself as you speak. Learn to speak in separate thoughts or ideas, one at a time. Leave a gap and a space for a thought to land with the other person. Always remember: what they are understanding is more important than what you are saying. If they are not understanding anything, there is no point in you continuing. As you leave that gap and watch it land with the other person, take a moment to see if they have taken it in or not. Wait, wait, wait to see if they have taken it in. If your thought has not landed with them (if they're frowning or looking vacant) then leave more space. This leaves a gap for them to interject. If they don't, then ask them if they need that explaining further. If your thought has in fact landed, then leave space for them to speak, and if they don't, you can either explain your point further or move on to the next one. We have so many conversations where we are delivering a download or a monologue and we don't even know where it ends. Then we start rambling. Never forget that anything worth saying is a dialogue, and the other person's contribution (even if that contribution is 'silent understanding') deserves equal space. Always leave room for pauses and for points to land. This is where understanding occurs. And this is where your status as a speaker soars.

- Think of a habit you want to change that affects your dominance. It could be that you hesitate to speak in meetings because you wait too long and when you're ready to speak the moment has passed. It could be that you find yourself physically slumping in meetings because you lose focus. It could be that you know you stumble over words when you speak. Whatever it is, identify one thing. Write it down. Now let it go and forget about it. At the same time, identify one behaviour – maybe a behaviour that you've noticed from a happy high status character on screen – that you wish you could use and make a note of it. It could be that you like the way Allison Janney enters a room as C. J. Cregg in *The West Wing*. Or the way Julianna Margulies holds her head as Alicia Florrick in *The Good Wife*. Or how Elisabeth Moss keeps a half-smile on her face when she is listening to someone as Peggy Olson in *Mad Men*. I am not asking you to copy these people or to sweep into a board meeting unannounced like you are Joan Collins in *Dynasty* circa 1985. But 'awareness is curative' and once you've identified it, this information starts to sink in. Even if you don't end up 'looking like' or 'being like' the character who has inspired you, you will gradually hold yourself in a different way. You are seeking – slowly, over time – to drop the habits and behaviours that annoy you in yourself: by identifying them, noting them, challenging them. And you are seeking to replace them with something different that feels fun and worth trying. Small change, big difference.

Inspiration for dominant happy high status: charismatic but deadly

Traits: Still, smooth body language. Charming. Charismatic. Can talk to anyone and make them feel like they're special. Direct talker. Engaged listener. Strong eye contact. Initiates in social situations instead of waiting for others to make their move.

Most useful for: Anyone who is shy and retiring and wants to play with the idea of being more assertive. To choose an extreme example can be liberating and fun.

Who succeeds at this (before a downfall): **Orson Welles as Charles Foster Kane in *Citizen Kane*** – in the early scenes he is (relatively) self-aware and has the world at his feet, brilliant at persuading others to listen. **Murray Bartlett as Armond in *The White Lotus*** – fabulously camp and controlling happy high status showcasing hospitality, warmth and dynamism before the slide into paranoia and disaster. **Lena Headey as Cersei Lannister in *Game of Thrones*** – power expressed as cool, serene stillness, carefully chosen words and intensely controlled facial

expressions. **Robin Wright as Claire Underwood in *House of Cards*** – a masterclass in quiet, elegant domination through intelligent charm and stylish Machiavellianism.
Michelle Yeoh as Philippa Georgiou in *Star Trek: Discovery* – extraordinarily layered and controlled depiction of varying gradations of soft and hard power, both menacing and persuasive.

Chapter 4

BE LIKE FINAL-SCENE SANDY AND DANNY

ON BEING NOT TOO COOL AND NOT TOO SELF-RIGHTEOUS

Balanced Happy High Status:
Charming and Benevolent

Escaping our childhood ideas of status

Our fear of coming across as 'too dominant' can hold us back from our confidence in adulthood. But so can hang-ups and misconceptions from adolescence, the time when most of us form our ideas around identity and self-assurance. In the ultimate teen movie, *Grease*, the characters Sandy Olsson (Olivia Newton-John) and Danny Zuko (John Travolta) are, like most teenagers, each trying to work out what kind of person they are: someone who leads or someone who follows. And they are trying to do this while staying true to themselves and not being fake. They are trying to be different kinds of happy high status, none of which are quite right for them, groping towards their own definition of grown-up, balanced happy high status. This everyday existential crisis forms the basis of any narrative of our teenage years and is the backdrop to the school experience for most of us, whether we conform to it or resist it. Are you in the 'in' crowd or the 'out' crowd? Or do you attempt to reject these categories? When we are at school, we either have to choose or we have this choice thrust upon us by others. Either way, it informs a big part of how we relate to our own confidence at a formative time in our lives.

Sandy and Danny illustrate key challenges for balanced happy high status that dog us from a young age: wanting to be liked and loved versus wanting to be aloof and respected; wanting to be one of the gang versus wanting to lead the gang; wanting recognition versus wanting to be able to remain unnoticed. At the start of the film, the song 'Summer Nights' ostensibly tells the story of a summer romance from two points of view. But really it's a status battle where they are each saying to the other: 'Why can't you be a bit more like me?' For both characters to become happy high status – which they (sort of) do by the end of the film – they need to borrow a little of the other's traits to be more balanced as individuals. He needs to be less narcissistic, worry less what others think of him and bow a little to conformity on occasion. We see this in the final fairground scene as he puts on the nerdy varsity jacket. He's trying. She needs to stand up for herself and rebel now and then. So she puts on a leather jacket. She's trying. These are baby steps towards the charm and benevolence of balanced happy high status: caring about others as much as you care about yourself. (Really not easy for teenagers.)

You see, the thing they both have in common here is that they are too worried – in different ways – about what others think. They are the epitome of self-consciousness. Danny wants others to think he is cool. Sandy wants others to think she is 'a good girl'. By the end of the film, they are both a little more like each other and so more like their 'real' selves. They do this by going to extremes: as well as the leather jacket, Sandy has to wear those ridiculous quasi-rubber trousers and start smoking to realize that she could do with loosening up a bit. (I very much doubt she would wear those trousers a second time. Apparently, Olivia Newton-John had to be cut out of them with scissors.)

In real life, as opposed to life at Rydell High, even if we accept that 'operating in a slightly different way' might be a good idea, we can still become trapped by wanting to be a version of ourselves that will be universally liked. Or at least not disliked. The importance of this has been drummed into us by society from a young age. At many stages of life, we become 'liked' by adjusting our status. Some people get their popularity from being high status ('the leader of the pack'). Others get their popularity and acceptance from being low status ('just one of the girls'). By the way, when I say 'low status' here, I don't mean that person is the lowest of the low. Sandy is clearly not that. I simply mean that they don't present a threat to others, they're not vying for position, they're a harmless member of the group.

In their initial incarnations, neither Sandy nor Danny is really happy high status. Sandy is too subservient, goody-two-shoes, naive and unaware of the bullying going on around her. She doesn't notice, for example, that her new 'friends' are undermining her. Even when she asks, 'Rizzo, are you mocking me?', she doesn't take action or walk away. Danny on the other hand is a fake. He plays the macho, alpha-male figure when he is with his friends: 'You know what it's like, babe. Rockin' and rollin' . . .' But we, the audience, know that they were both different people when they were with each other during their summer romance. We see that Sandy is *capable of being higher status* and is keeping herself 'low' for no good reason other than wanting to fit in. And we see that Danny's perceived 'high status' is actually rather fraudulent. She could do with being higher. He could do with being lower. Even though Olivia Newton-John was twenty-eight and John Travolta was twenty-three when they played these roles, they are portraying a typical kind of teenage status conflict that can play out in one of three ways: 1) Not knowing what your status really is, 2) Pretending that your status is more than it is, and 3) Choosing to remain low status and taking 'victim' as your identity. Most of us grow out of this, but some of us stay trapped in it our whole lives, either imagining that we are 'less than' (3), puffing out our chests and feigning being 'more than' (2), or oscillating between the two (1). Ultimate happy high status is when you make your peace with all three of these states and find your own balance.

This isn't the ideal example, seeing as the lesson of *Grease* could be summed up as: 'The way to be popular is to pretend to be a completely different person, ideally one who smokes and wears very tight trousers.' But we will set that to one side for now and look at the broader message: the perception of our status that we developed in adolescence does not define us – we can 'stretch' our status whenever we want to come across slightly differently. And we don't have to conform to a childish or simplistic picture of what that looks like. When I think of Sandy in that leather jacket, I am reminded of the career women in the 1980s and 1990s wearing men's suits for the boardroom. Putting on a leather jacket and smoking a cigarette does not really make you sexy and grown-up. Wearing a suit and saying 'Let's look at these year-end figures' in a deep voice does not really give you authority and status. That's not to say that your outward appearance makes no difference at all. It's just that if it doesn't match up with your behaviour, intentions and genuine status – as experienced on the inside (by you) and on the outside (by others) – then the first impression will last about as long as those teeny tiny trousers.

Status, identity and authority

We can form ideas early in our lives – often influenced by family labels – as to who we are in terms of identity and as to where our status lies. We also form opinions early on about how we relate to the status of others. Some people make it their business to respect authority. Others kick against it. We can feel ambiguous about authority depending on our personal history and whether we were treated well or badly by the authority figures in our lives. My point is not that there is a right or a wrong way to feel about authority or status, simply that we all have an attitude towards it, whether we realize it or not. And that attitude is going to affect how we inhabit status ourselves.

Many of these early ideas about what it means to be confident, to hold authority, to be a leader and to be looked up to are formed at school. This is one reason why the concepts of status and power can feel incredibly daunting, off-putting and even contradictory. From childhood, we are conditioned to respect status but also to suspect it and, at times, even to ridicule it. Yes, you obey a teacher and do what they say. But do that too much and you are a 'teacher's pet'. As individuals we respect authority to intensely differing degrees. Some of us will behave as if a teacher is in charge no matter what the circumstances and do the right 'socially acceptable' thing. But some of us will do 'the wrong thing' as soon as the teacher's back is turned, especially if we know we definitely won't get caught. Our attitude towards authority figures can make us resistant to holding any kind of authority ourselves.

If you were bullied by a teacher (or a parent) or your older sibling made your life a misery, or your boss at your first job was a Machiavellian, conniving rat, you are probably going to react in a certain way when you take status yourself. For some people, that awareness is going to make them more respectful of status because they know what it means to see it abused. For others, they are simply going to walk away from it or sabotage that opportunity because they won't want to associate themselves in their own mind with that bully figure.

Experience and identity form us as individuals and

those two factors have different weightings in different people. For example, in *Grease* we don't know if Danny has older or younger siblings. He could have an older brother who he is trying to live up to by being 'cool'. He could have been bullied and adopted his 'coolness' as a defence. Or he could simply be an only child who wants to adopt this identity because it feels right to him. (In any case, I am enjoying my elevation to Danny Zuko's psychotherapist.) This is a simplistic explanation of a complex phenomenon that would play out in each of us differently. What matters is to think about where you sit on this continuum. What is your attitude towards status? Do you resist it or embrace it? Does it sit well in you? Can you tolerate others when they take status? In psychology, the term 'acting out' is used to mean 'communicating what cannot be verbalized'. Sometimes we 'act out' (by being falsely modest, by being confident in a fake way, by refusing to do things that seem to require confidence) because we cannot verbalize certain truths: 'I don't want people to think I'm a show-off.' 'I don't want anyone to know that I secretly feel insecure.' 'I can face anything except humiliation.' Once we admit that we're saying these things to ourselves, we can make progress.

Bringing the ghost of our teenage selves to work

Balanced happy high status is about being aware of these things, and using that knowledge to adjust to our own foibles and tendencies and to adjust to those around us. I see this play out in very interesting ways when people are talking about public speaking or presenting, in relation to audience size. These attitudes weirdly mimic the scenarios that play out in *Grease* or any other depiction of school life. Some people find their status is threatened when an authority figure is in the room. Some are intimidated by an audience of people they know well. ('I don't want my friend/colleague to sit in the front row' or 'I can't do it unless my friend/colleague sits in the front row.') Others hate to be put up in front of a group of strangers. People also form fascinating ideas about when they can 'hide' or feel comfortable. I've heard all these variations: 'I'm OK in front of five people but not ten.' 'I hate speaking one-to-one face-to-face but I'm fine presenting to the whole company on Zoom.' 'I can speak to a group of a hundred people, no problem, but I hate doing pitches in a room of five people where I can see all their facial expressions.' We don't mean to reveal our teenage selves with these complaints. But here they are.

Some of these reactions are about nerves and getting used to managing your nerves in different contexts. We all know the most useful and obvious tips here: practice, preparation and breathing. That kind of practical advice works when your confidence is reasonably good and you just need a little extra support to calm yourself. But some of our reactions in these situations are more deep-seated and reflect our individual hang-ups around authority and status. Without psychoanalysing every individual, I imagine these kinds of limiting beliefs stem back to something from childhood or school days. If you hate your boss being in the room, maybe you had one teacher who was really harsh on you. If you hate speaking to a group, maybe you had a negative experience in class at school. These things can have echoes for years – and for no good reason because, hurtful though they are, they are almost always more about the circumstances (that teacher was a bully, that class was poorly controlled) than they are about something lacking in you. These expressions of fear also relate to ideas that we receive when we are younger: that people can easily 'put you off' while you are doing things, and that the good opinion of onlookers is the main factor in success. Once you are in a state of happy high status, you do not care about these things or notice them. Part of that is about acknowledging these factors and being aware of them. We can't undo what was done to us in the past. But we can be aware that it is still influencing us and understand that the influence is not helpful, so we might want to think about changing it.

Being balanced happy high status is about being 'not too cool' (early-stage Danny) and 'not too self-righteous' (early-stage Sandy). The 'coolness' is too inauthentic to be happy high status: it depends too much on the opinion of others. The self-righteousness is too smug to be happy high status: it reflects an excessive opinion of the self. Perhaps most of all, it is about balance and accommodation. Care about others but not too much (so that others do not take advantage of you). Believe in yourself but not to excess (so that you do not take advantage of others). It is about being comfortable with your particular position in the world, whatever position you happen to be occupying at that moment. You can assert yourself, but you can also yield. You can take charge, but you can also take orders. You don't respond to things in a reactive way because you need everyone to think that you are a dude (Danny) or because you need everyone to think that you always get everything right (Sandy). You respond to things with proportion and common sense. Most of all – and this is going to sound very annoying but it sums it up – care deeply while being carefree. Yes, I know this sounds impossible. Another way to express this? Invest deeply in things but then let go of the outcome.

I particularly notice the pull towards self-righteousness or 'coolness' in people when they are preparing for public speaking. There is the desire to be right, to be unquestionable, to be unassailable. And there is the desire to be liked, admired, revered. Many people really struggle to relinquish any control or let in any spontaneity. This can suddenly be revealed, for example, if you talk about taking a Q&A after a speech. Some people will say: 'I don't like Q&As because I might be asked something and I won't know the answer.' But we are not at Rydell High any more. You are not going to get a C-minus on the test. In real life we often don't know the answer. Or it could be that the question isn't a great question. Or the answer lies outside your expertise or your remit. What is really being revealed here is this: 'I don't want anyone to make me look bad (or "uncool"). I want to be confident enough to always be right.' But confidence is not about always being right and always having the answer. True confidence is not knowing, being uncertain or deferring to someone else and being OK with that. Of course, if the truth is you don't know the answer because you haven't really prepared or you're not up to the job then that is not a question of confidence, it is a question of diligence and competence. The balanced happy high status response to realizing you're out of your depth is finding an elegant way to cover that up, and making sure that you become more diligent and competent in future. Or getting a job that is more suited to you. It's not about bullshitting your way through to try to look good.

Confidence is in the eye of the beholder

When we are rooting out our teenage ideas about status and replacing them with something more useful, we immediately come up against the subjective nature of confidence and happy high status. Often when I am explaining this to people, I can see that they don't feel comfortable relying on their own ideas about what 'feels like' leadership or what 'looks like' status. They want concrete, transactional rules that lead to tangible results: 'Behave like this and they will give you a promotion.' 'Hold your head like this and people will think you're a good speaker.' 'Breathe in and out this number of times and everyone will think you are super-confident.' This is nonsense, of course, but we are drawn to believe that there is a secret code that you can crack, and then everything will come to you.

Another thing people don't really want to hear about confidence is that you can have as much of it as you want and some people around you still won't buy it. Confidence is a bit like pleasing people. You can please some of the people some of the time but you can't please all of the people all of the time. This is what my father told me repeatedly during the 1980s. It was a trademark parenting mantra at the time. It has transformed in the twenty-first century into 'Haters gonna hate.' More broadly put: confidence reads differently on everyone and there is no objective measure of its success. It comes back to the crucial point: really, you are the only person who can truly know if you are confident or not. This is way beyond the 'popularity contest' definition of confidence most of us will have witnessed in our teens.

This is a profound idea that we rarely discuss. When confidence is in the eye of the beholder, nothing is objectively beautiful and no one is objectively confident. This is the painful reality reflected in the song 'Summer Nights'. Both Sandy and Danny thought they met a special person that summer. But in the cold light of the new school term, their experience turns out to be highly subjective. They were both pretty confident in that relationship (even if they each have a different view of what went on). But once they're in a different setting, it turns out their confidence is misplaced. The magical quality they once somehow beheld in each other has evaporated.

Many things are in the eye of the beholder: attractive-
ness, intelligence, authority . . . You might think, 'That's
not right. I can immediately see for a fact if someone is
confident or not.' But what's true for us might not be true
for everyone. Most of the time we rely extensively on our
abilities as subjective beholders rather than on facts. Does
this person *seem* beautiful to me? Does this person carry
what I take to be authority? Does this person *come across* as
intelligent? We read people and situations, and we draw
conclusions. But just as we don't all read a book the same
way, we don't 'read' people the same way, either. For anyone who wants to use happy high status as a principle to
improve the way they come across, it is essential that they
accept this. You can work really hard on your confidence,
your self-presentation, on everything about yourself, and
there will always be people on whom it simply does not
work. Even Danny and Sandy are not universally attractive to everyone. Nonetheless we believe very strongly in
our abilities as 'beholders'. We know deep down that these
judgements are subjective, but we convince ourselves that,
because we have seen it and felt it and 'know' it, our subjective evaluation is in fact objective. This thing really is
beautiful. This person really does have authority. That
behaviour is a true projection of confidence.

Why am I asking you to think about this? Because no
two definitions of confidence will be the same and the only
person who can know whether yours is 'real' is you. For
some people, supreme, glorious, show-stopping confidence is completely fake. Many film stars, comedians and

performers achieve their allure by being confident or – as we usually call it – charismatic. But there is no one whose charisma works on the entire population. Naturally, some of those who don't buy into the charms of these beguiling souls are kidding themselves: they're rejecting someone's charisma just because they're envious. They secretly recognize their appeal. But for others, their befuddlement is real. They really do think, 'What's the deal with . . . [insert name of conventionally attractive or popular person whose popularity you don't understand]? I just don't get it.' No one is universally loved, universally believed to be beautiful, universally charismatic. So it makes sense that confidence – a highly subjective quality that is even difficult to put into words, more of a feeling than anything else – would be something indefinite and nebulous. The sooner you get used to this idea, the sooner you can work on the kind of confidence that feels real to you.

This is not intended to sound depressing. On the contrary, it is liberating. Because it means we can all create our own version of how confidence is defined. Perhaps it would be comforting if there were some kind of one-size-fits-all confidence toolkit with a money-back guarantee. You could learn those skills and tricks, and your problems would be solved (and yes, of course, to some extent they do exist in some measure and yes, this book is suggesting some of those things). But the thing is, even then you might not always feel confident in all situations. And even if you did, not everyone would 'buy' your confidence. If this seems unfair or disappointing then just think about a popular actor or pop star who everyone seems to like apart from you. This person has confidence and that confidence reads successfully for a lot of people a lot of the time. But it didn't work on you. This, then, is a process of deep self-trust and self-reliance, learning to be honest with yourself and kind to yourself – and finding the time and space to experiment in order to find what works for you, without having to rely on someone else to tell you you're OK. This is true balanced happy high status: when you've weighed yourself up in your own mind and decided that you're just about right. And when you feel that way, charm and benevolence cannot help but follow.

How to get a piece of it

- The opposite of teen awkwardness is looking and feeling comfortable in your own body. If you can just come across as 'at ease' in your own body, that is half the battle. Non-verbal communication is the thing to look at when studying examples of balanced or charming happy high status. Typical hallmarks: predictability and ease of movement, relaxed stillness, fluid physicality. This is why people who are physically fit or have great mobility often come across as confident externally even when they may not be internally. (And why

dancers do not need to say a word: we read
their confidence non-verbally.) Keeping relaxed
and still – as in 'calm', not 'frozen' – is the
quickest way to increase your status. In any
speech or performance you can use movement
at different points but you need to think about
why you're moving. Are you doing it to make a
point? To change the subject? To indicate a
different upcoming mood? To draw a line under
something you've finished saying? To shift the
audience's attention away from a bit where you
messed up? To reset the room because it's
lacking in energy? These are all good reasons to
move across a stage or change position. Bad
reasons? Because you feel nervous and fidgety.
Because you don't know what else to do.
Because you wish you weren't there. Because
you don't know what to do with your hands
when you're speaking. Because you can't stop
pacing.

• The basic physical hallmarks of mature,
considered happy high status are calmness,
openness and symmetry. Some people seem
to interpret this wrongly: they think they will
come across as more 'senior' or 'like a leader'
if they are stiff or formal. Instead, think about

'focus' (your own and the audience's). And be kind to yourself: it takes time to learn how to hold space without looking like C-3PO. When people first start trying to discipline themselves to be more still and more symmetrical on stage or on camera, they can't help doing it in a way that is unnatural. That's normal, so don't blame yourself and get angry if at first it feels weird. Once you do it often enough, it becomes second nature. I don't believe for a moment that any newsreaders or TV presenters think about this kind of thing for a second, or would be able to explain anything about status, but they *know it in their bones.* It's muscle memory for them. Watch out, in particular, for the relatively new trend of TV newsreaders standing up to present, often next to a wall graphic. They will stand with their weight evenly planted, not slouching and not leaning to one side (as we tend to do in normal life). They will use hand and arm gestures only sparingly, if at all. They will hold their hands in such a way that they do not draw attention: this might mean them physically holding a finger or a thumb and not moving their hands at all. All these traits enhance stillness, and when we have stillness in our body, the audience is able to concentrate on our facial expressions and our words, and really take in what we're saying.

• Think about 'range'. There is a world of difference between 'being something that you're not' and 'trying something different'. Actors don't want to be pigeonholed as a particular type of person. Nor do they want their characters to be monodimensional in their emotions. So they learn how to play low status and high status. They learn how to laugh and cry on command. Without trying to make everyone into an actor, how amazing would it be if we could all have the 'range' that we need in life? In terms of social ability, confidence, emotional flexibility? But without faking it and without needing to be paid and get awards for doing it. (Sorry to actors. You deserve all the money and all the awards. There's a brilliant Jane Fonda quote that sums this up: 'We all, in fact, carry so many people inside us. The only difference is that actors get paid for it and we sort of spruce it up a bit.') You can always experiment, go too far and row back. Even if you are already confident in most situations, you can still expand your range so that you are more confident in even more situations. Ask yourself if you can really stretch your range and allow yourself to be so confident that you can display vulnerability. If 'range' is too actor-ly a word for you, think of it as bandwidth. How can you stretch your emotional bandwidth?

Inspiration for balanced happy high status: charming and benevolent

Traits: Likeable. Attractive. Kind. Trustworthy. Equally capable of leading and following. Can bring levity when necessary and seriousness when required. Someone other people gravitate towards. Sensitive and empathic without being introverted. Makes other people feel comfortable. Doesn't make it about themselves.

Most useful for: People who are inclined towards self-consciousness. This provides a model for looking outwards and looking after other people. Useful for anyone who finds they are often taken advantage of and could do with standing up for themselves a bit more.

Who succeeds at this: **James Stewart as George Bailey in *It's a Wonderful Life*** – when George is experiencing good times, no one is more happy high status. (His status in bad times is a perfect example of the mafia-style dominant variant.) **Meg Ryan as Sally and Billy Crystal as Harry in *When Harry Met Sally*** – we see them moving up and down in status throughout this film and ultimately ending up as the perfect happy high status match for each other. **Julie Andrews as Maria in *The Sound of Music*** – a character who is too happy high status to be true, who endures a lessening of status and the exposure of her flaws before finding her true happy high status self. **Carrie Fisher as Princess Leia in *Star Wars*** – raised to be regal and yet underneath 'ordinary', Leia has to learn how to carry herself with dignity and grace without coming across as overbearing. **Michael J. Fox as Marty McFly in *Back to the Future*** – a great example of 'cute' happy high status combining charisma with a dose of wide-eyed naivety.

Chapter 5

BE LIKE CLOONEY ON TEQUILA DUTY

ENTITLEMENT, STEREOTYPES AND REINVENTION

Generous Happy High Status:
Grounded Magnanimity

'God give me the confidence of a mediocre white dude.' – Sarah Hagi

Let us return to the story of George Clooney following behind you with your drink at the imaginary Oscars party. It is a useful one for explaining generous happy high status superficially and quickly. It's a memorable form of shorthand and it bears repeating because it stays in the mind's eye. And not just the mind's eye of an addled middle-aged mother of three. The principle behind it is reminiscent of the famous quote attributed to Eleanor Roosevelt: 'No one can make you feel inferior without your consent.' But it is also a good way into discussing some of the complications of happy high status as well as some of the hesitations some of us might have in adopting it as a confidence strategy. Because . . . Well, how do I put this? There two issues staring us in the face here. First, only one person is George Clooney, and that is George Clooney. And second, this story reflects a stereotype.

Someone like George Clooney is an example of why many people find the idea of confidence not inspiring and motivating but off-putting and intimidating. The man is, by definition and surely from birth, generous, magnanimous, grounded. How are any of us supposed to live up to that? How is any of this achievable? Is it even worth bothering? Indeed, you may well be thinking, 'Viv, this theory is all very well for people who are up on stage or who are Oscar-winning actors. But how is this supposed to help me? Because I am not planning to move to Hollywood or join a comedy improv group any time soon. Nor do I want to make a television commercial for a popular brand of coffee pod which seems to reflect the version of George Clooney you are talking about and is rapidly becoming outdated as a cultural trope. You might want to think about that.' Also, women may be thinking, 'I can never be George Clooney as I am a woman. Why couldn't you put a woman in this example?'

In all my positivity and enthusiasm around this theory, it has to be acknowledged that there is a huge issue at the heart of this basic illustration of happy high status. And it's not only that this Oscars-party story is entirely fictional and we may all only live it in our dreams. (Although, by the way, it turns out that this story is in some ways slowly coming true. Not only did George Clooney play a waiter in *Murder, She Wrote* in 1984, he also apparently made a habit of dating cocktail waitresses in his early bachelor life. He then went on to found the tequila company Casamigos. Tequila! Plus he allegedly loves playing bartender at high-end events, including the wedding of the Duke and Duchess of Sussex, at which he is supposed to have handed out shots. Among all these waiter-adjacent activities, it's amazing he has any time for acting or directing. I mean, I'm not saying that I'm willing this made-up story into being but . . . It could've happened. It might yet happen. George Clooney himself is undeniably making moves towards it happening.)

But, yes. Let's get back to the problem. Of course, this story is fake and imaginary. Perhaps worse than being fake, it reinforces a really big, fat, obvious stereotype. It evokes a trope that has been popular in movies and fiction since the dawn of time: the suave, elegant gentleman who is unflappable, impossible to humiliate, who always comes out on top, who always has a bon mot, who always gets the girl. Of course, that git is generous happy high status. It's Clooney, James Bond, Mr Darcy, James Stewart, Cary Grant . . . Add in your preferred clichéd definition of lead-ing man here. So if you are starting to bristle and are quite rightly thinking, 'Well, it's all right for George Clooney,' then I agree. Sceptical readers should and will raise an eye-brow over this cute trope about an attractive man who has the world at his feet. I know I would.

You don't have to be Daniel Craig playing a detective in *Knives Out* – hey, there's someone else who is effort-lessly generous happy high status – to notice what all Clooney and his stand-ins have in common. They are men, they are white, they are privileged. (Usually also wealthy, famous, intelligent, physically strong, handsome, heteronormative, not working class . . .) In short, they occupy an enviable position in the world. Let's face it: it couldn't be easier for them to be happy high status. The world imbues them with effortless confidence from birth. All they have to do is move through it with a smile on their perfectly symmetrical faces. What about the rest of us, who aren't rich and famous, who didn't get even invited to that party, who might be real-life waiters and waitresses, who don't tick all those boxes? How are we supposed to be happy high status? Aren't the odds stacked against us from the start? How are we, without their advantages, supposedly to become the soul of grounded magnanimity?

Refusing permission to feel inferior

The thing is, if we don't automatically tick the boxes society has prepared for us over many millennia, sometimes we just have to tick the boxes for ourselves. But confidence is not an easy inside job. That famous quote imploring us to ignore anyone who makes us feel inferior has always fascinated me. It makes sense and is logical. But imagine saying it to a child who is being bullied: 'No one can make you feel small unless you let them.' It is not supposed to be deflating and depressing. But it is. It actually sounds dismissive rather than reassuring or inspiring. It's reminiscent of that ultimate supposed confidence-boosting saying that does not work at all: 'Sticks and stones may break my bones but names will never hurt me.' Easy to say. Not so easy to believe deep inside.

These sayings have arisen as a reminder to us that we are bigger than the people who seek to bring us down, and that our own internal estimation of ourselves deserves to be unbreakable and not dependent on others. But these 'don't let the bastards get you down'-type sayings are more about the perpetrator, whether that person is intentionally or unintentionally hurtful – the bully, the name-caller, the chump who has mistaken George Clooney for a waiter – than they are about the person on the receiving end of the perceived insult. These sayings remind us that the person who started this is the real problem. But that is not much consolation when they have just socked your self-esteem in the stomach. How do you really believe these sayings and genuinely believe in yourself, rather than just pay lip service to the idea? How do you generously walk away mentally from situations that rattle your confidence when you are not an alpha born with the personality equivalent of a silver spoon?

I've had a lot of challenging responses to this Clooney story, and from women especially. They get the point, they get the story. They want to understand how to shrug off a slight in a way that is elegant and cool. They want to be graceful in the face of disaster, ridicule and PowerPoint breakdown. In their head they may be trying to convince themselves: 'I give no one permission to make me feel inferior.' But the trouble is, something like this has happened to them in real life and there was no George Clooney laugh-it-off resolution. In reality their heart is in pain and for good reason. At an event for women who work in finance, a young Black woman told me: 'I get the George Clooney story totally. I get why you are telling it. And I get that in life we can choose how we react to how we are treated. But I have been mistaken for the coat-check person at work events on so many occasions by people who are supposed to be my colleagues or are even junior to me. What am I meant to do in that situation?' Why, in that situation, should she be the one to strive for generous happy high status?

She's absolutely right to ask that. Clooney might have picked up the drink and ferried it over with a smile on his face. But, in the case of this young woman, if you are mistaken for the coat-check person, you need a swift intervention, otherwise you are soon going to end up buried under a mountain of coats. Or you are going to need to call out your colleagues in a way that is fundamentally uncomfortable and maybe even potentially dangerous for your career. The fact is, a woman – alongside anyone from an under-represented group – could easily be in this situation in real life because it is generally *assumed* that their status is lower than it is. It's easy to look at a scenario like this from the outside and shout, 'She is not the coat-check person! She is the head of finance! Stop making racist and sexist assumptions!' But when you are inside this situation, it is not easy to shout this.

Assumptions are hard to challenge, as often they're based on generalizations. These likelihoods are stuck fast in our brains and they are tough to remove, especially as we're often not explicitly aware that we're making these assumptions (hence the terms 'unconscious bias' and 'internalized misogyny' – just to introduce a fun note).

This means that, with the best will in the world, assumptions are made about status based on conjecture and subconscious guesswork rather than fact and careful consideration. The world would be a very different place if we began every face-to-face encounter with the thought, 'What if this person is a CEO?' But unfortunately, statistically in most parts of the Western world, if you are not a white man of a certain age who looks a certain way then there is a likelihood that you will not be the highest status person in the room. Statistically most women are not the boss. Statistically the person doing the coffee run really will be a woman. Statistically women are still more likely to be secretaries than CEOs. (I know. It hurt me to write that sentence. Facts are irritating.)

Anyone can be happy high status *in theory*. But in reality, as the George Clooney story suggests, there are specific qualities and assumptions that go towards elevating someone's status. And those qualities have traditionally been more recognized and rewarded among certain demographics. Yes, that stereotype is changing fast. But it is still powerful, and it is frequently the elephant in the room when it comes to thinking about happy high status. There is still a widespread belief that 'some people' get a free pass when it comes to confidence, and so when we start to consider our own confidence, we're already thinking about it with a certain amount of resentment and hopelessness. This is a big stumbling block for a lot of people, and especially for women. I'm not saying that I like this fact or that I defend it or excuse it. But it is real. We unconsciously project the most confidence and the most status on to the people who are historically the most likely to have those things.

To acknowledge this means to start thinking about equality, diversity, gender, race, class, poverty and inter-sectionality (defined as the overlapping and interdependency of systems of discrimination or disadvantage). If that does not sound very fun, it's because it isn't – and it's also a rea-son why people can become very angry when talking about leadership, power, money, opportunities and, yes, confidence. Put simply, we are not all born looking like George Clooney nor have we all had his advantages or good fortune in life. (Which is not to suggest for a second that George Clooney does not deserve his achievements. He is an enviably talented and demonstrably hard-working individual. Just call me, George. Call, OK?) However, as I'm sure someone of George Clooney's sensibility and intellect would be the first to acknowledge, this same 'fol-low me with the cocktail' story would be very different if it were about a woman, even in the twenty-first century. It also would have a very different message if the case of mis-taken identity were about someone who was not white, as the message would centre around racial discrimination. Or if it were about someone with a disability. I won't go on. Because you see what I mean.

Whether we like it or not, power dynamics are at work in almost every situation in life that we encounter, and we respect them unconsciously all the time whether we mean to or not. There is a communal understanding of what this pantomime represents. This is why the same story doesn't work for women, as it would be very unlikely a) that you would mistake a waitress for a guest because of dress codes (dress code itself being another kind of stereotype), and b) if you did and it was, let's say, Meryl Streep, it would be very difficult for her to maintain the poise required for this interaction because your mistake would be profoundly weird. (Although, OK, yes, I'm pretty sure Meryl Streep could carry it off.) But the context of the story matters because it represents a stereotype that people can easily recognize. My point is this: you can recognize the panto-mime. And you can make sure you step out of it and – with generosity – play the part you want to play.

How do you get past stereotypes and make people see you as an individual?

If I had an easy answer to this question, I would be a very wealthy woman and possibly empress of the cosmos. Instead, I am a great believer in the old therapeutic adage that you cannot change other people's behaviour if they don't want to change it themselves. The only person whose behaviour you can change is your own. By which I mean in this instance that unfortunately you can't force people to get past stereotypes if they don't want to. You cannot make them be generous. You can only decide to embrace your own generosity. In theory, there ought to be a global anti-bias training module that everyone on Earth should undertake so that we can all stop making assumptions about everything. When I become empress, I will make it law. Perhaps everyone who passes the training could have the words 'Assume nothing' stamped on their forehead. Perhaps people could learn to say, 'Oh dear. I know I have just asked you to take my coat because I decided that statistically there is a strong possibility that someone who looks like you is responsible for the coat-check. I will attempt in future to move beyond statistics and un-conscious bias and think about you as an individual. I apologize.' In reality, we don't have the capacity to roll out this training to everyone on the planet and I am not going to become empress. So instead we have no choice but to accept that a lot of human beings will often make assumptions.

You can challenge those assumptions, of course. And if you're thinking that you don't resent being the person who says, 'Excuse me, you seem to have mistaken me for a waiter/coffee-maker/coat-check person and I am, in fact, the global head of human resources,' then I bow to you and wish you good luck. Sometimes this needs saying and is not a waste of breath. But sometimes this stance is pointless. Plus, a lot of people will not want to do this because it will make them feel awkward. Or they just can't be bothered.

The other solutions for maintaining poise? Well, the situation does leave room for choice and creativity. But also for resigned dignity. Sometimes confidence is loud and demonstrative. Other times it is sober and pragmatic. In her book *The Light We Carry: Overcoming in Uncertain Times*, Michelle Obama tells the childhood story of her father's car being scratched all down the side when the family went to a dinner in a predominantly white neighbourhood. Her father's reaction – which arguably is a generous happy high status reaction at any time and certainly for its time historically – was to be what Michelle Obama calls 'a withholder'. He withheld his anger, held his head high and sucked it up. He did not seek to challenge the situation. This reaction is surely at the root of what is meant by 'When they go low, we go high.' Which is itself another way of saying, 'Turn the other cheek.' This is what I mean when I say that magnanimity is not generic, it is individual and subjective and it is open to interpretation.

Our individual reactions to this are instructive and they hold the key to understanding that confidence comes in many different guises. Sometimes generous happy high status is confrontation and speaking truth to power in a calm, clear voice. Sometimes it is when you glower and simmer and almost lose it, but ultimately walk away. Other times it means simply shrugging and ignoring something. The essence of generous happy high status is to find in every situation what this response looks like for you and what sits right with you. It's not up to any of us to judge what others do in this situation. But it is up to each of us to find a way to respond to situations in a way that makes us feel like we did the right thing. The real job of confidence is not to find someone who can tell you what the most confident response is. It's to decide what it is for yourself.

Using generous happy high status to go from 'what is' to 'what could be'

'What is' represents the stereotype: 'the way things are' right now or the status quo. It often follows the dominant power structures. It's our automatic response to a situation, or our subconscious assumption about how the world works. It's the default in a world where not everyone is familiar with the expression 'unconscious bias'. It's possible to argue that not everyone buys that stereotype of 'what is' or 'the way things are', not everyone sees the same story, not everyone buys into the same myth. And yes, of course, many people make it their business to question the status quo or they simply don't conform to it. Of course, there are rebels out there. For example, not everyone loves George Clooney. Arguably he's rapidly ageing out of being perfect for the role of the fake waiter in this story anyway, and maybe it's time to replace him with Ryan Gosling. Or even Harry Styles. Or Rylan. Let's make him Rylan. (Now that I come to think of it: sorry, George, but you are way too old to be a waiter now.)

So it's entirely reasonable to argue that the fake-waiter-figure-who-turns-out-to-be-charming-celebrity-role-model-for-happy-high-status *should and could be* anyone of any race or any age or any gender. Someone who is used to examining unconscious bias could certainly argue that. However. 'What is' is not the same as 'what should be' or 'what could be'. There is simply no denying that the George

Clooney story tells us something about 'the way things are' and 'what is'. There are thousands of studies that show that most of us, whether we mean to or not, are swayed by stereotypes, bias and snap decisions, all of which are – completely understandably, if tragically – informed by centuries of cultural conditioning. We all know in real life 'what is'. We know that certain kinds of people are more likely to find themselves mistaken for a waiter than others. And that some people are more able to laugh off a social faux pas than others. We all know about the thousands of bias studies which show that if you talk to a group of people about 'the boss', most of them will – unconsciously – picture a man. Same goes for 'scientist', 'doctor', 'surgeon' and on. And you could do the same study with 'nursery teacher', 'primary school teacher' or 'nanny', and they will no doubt picture a woman. We have all heard about the research that has been done on blind job applications where if it's a woman's name or someone with a 'foreign-sounding' surname, the outcome is less favourable than if the CV belongs to John Smith. (I know. So depressing. Why are human beings so basic?)

We all know the news headlines about the sector of government and big business where there are 'more men called Dave or [insert generic-white-man's-name-here] than women' in the top jobs. There are loads of variations on this gem. From 2005: 'There are more men called David than women in the shadow cabinet.' From 2014: 'There are more men called Dave or Steve than there are women standing for election for UKIP.' (Yes, I know it's

UKIP so not remotely surprising, but still.) From 2015: 'There are more men called Nigel than women on the government's select committee.' From 2018: 'There are more men called David than there are women leading FTSE 100 companies.' (In 2015 it was John.) And we all know that any research like this is going to give the same results if you put race, disability, identity, to some extent age, or anything you like underneath the microscope, instead of gender. The point is not to ask: 'Do these things really happen?' Clearly they do and, yes, it is getting boring even talking about it. Nor even: 'Why do these things happen?' Answer: centuries of cultural conditioning. These things happened for historical reasons that at the time were logical or unavoidable. It may not be right that things developed this way, and often the logic was fuelled by ignorance, oppression, violence or all three. But they happened. And they inform people's current assumptions.

The point is to ask: What next? What do we do with this information, once we've pointed it out and moaned about it? The version of happy high status that I want to argue for finds a space for 'what could be'. That is the only generous solution. The only thing that can affect what happens next is if we behave differently and support others who are also behaving differently. There is a direct correlation between the 'Dave' headlines and the fact that George Clooney works as the ultimate stereotype in this illustration of status. It is unfortunately true that for a long time confidence, leadership and power have been correlated with a certain stereotype. So if you don't feel naturally confident, this could well be part of the reason. There's no point in pretending that this is not the case. It's also true that there are plenty of 'mediocre white men' (blame Sarah Hagi for this expression, not me . . .) who are actually very nice and deserving people, and who feel – with good reason – that they have been overlooked in some regard or have never quite been able to work out how to sell themselves or who have had a lot of setbacks in life. I imagine there are days when even George Clooney is not very much like George Clooney. Each of us needs to be able to take a deep breath, remove Clooney and Co. out of that example, insert ourselves and imagine our own version of generous happy high status. Maybe we'll do it so well that we'll completely redefine what it looks like. (Sorry, George, that's another job you've lost. You'll get over it.)

What is a waste of time on a day-to-day individual level, though, is stressing out about other people's assumptions and about human stupidity, which is something that is impossible to change overnight and on your own. The solution is to ask practically, radically, creatively: 'What reaction here will make me feel more confident? What reaction helps me sleep better at night?' You can choose to feel annoyed, defeated, belittled, frustrated. Or you can choose to recognize that this has nothing to do with you personally and everything to do with the last gazillion years of human history. Remove resentment from your feelings about your own confidence. Choose instead generosity. Choose grounded magnanimity.

How to get a piece of it

- A major step to channelling generous happy high status more often is figuring out in advance what your self-assured response will be when your confidence is challenged or shaken. Question yourself: 'How do I respond under pressure?' 'What is my reaction when my status is challenged?' 'Am I protecting my ego?' 'If I put that hurt to one side, what options do I have?' But it's also important to be realistic about the interactions that we face. Taking generous happy high status as a guideline is useful: 'What is the "bigger person" response?' It could be to turn the other cheek, to rise above it, to go high. It could be to weigh up the cost of an emotional reaction. Does it benefit you to become angry? Or does it benefit you to keep your cool? Do you need to reframe it and take it less personally? What's the exhausting, debilitating emotional cost of responding to every single slight with rage? The generous happy high status response is to take a step back, de-escalate the emotions and think, 'What is the best outcome for me?'

- Buy time in any stressful situation. You can always respond: 'Let me get back to you on that.' Or sometimes no response is a way of saying the same thing. You can always say: 'I don't have a response to that right now. Give me a moment.' The moment can take thirty seconds or a week. It takes time to know how to respond in the way that suits us best. Many situations that are a direct challenge to our confidence are exacerbated because there is a perceived time pressure. 'I need to hit back right now otherwise the other person will have won.' No. Buy time. Wait. Consider.

- Whose generous happy high status would you like to role-model? Make a list. Not in an attempt to copy them, exactly, but in an attempt to think more about what your own version of that kind of confidence looks like. The term 'role model' is constructed that way for a reason. We all inhabit 'roles' just as actors do, and the term 'role model' is asking us to consider the kind of 'role' we want to play. Who is that for you? And who is it definitely not? Don't confuse this kind of role model with someone whose job you might want to have or whose success you might want to emulate.

Think of behavioural or 'energy' role models. Who has good energy? Who is listened to in a way you would want to be listened to? Who handles people in a way that you appreciate? Tip: this is more likely to bring to mind people that you have met in real life than celebrities. But any role models are relevant and tell you something about what you're trying to achieve. Remember: generous happy high status is a mode of breezy calm. It's an internal shrug that does not betray any passive aggression. You are looking for people who can do that.

Inspiration for generous happy high status: grounded magnanimity

Traits: Larger than life. Openly charming. Occasionally non-conformist. Happy to stand out from the crowd. Wears points of difference, flaws and insecurities as a badge of honour. Defiant in the face of haters. At ease with multiple viewpoints. In-your-face but doesn't have to be right about everything.

Most useful for: People who are tired of trying to fit in and are ready to lead others. Anyone who either has a thick skin or is willing to develop a thick skin. Reformed narcissists who like showing off but want to do their showing off in service of something bigger than themselves.

Who succeeds at this: **Harry Styles** – singer who treats his own image with a sense of humour and does his own thing. **Ashley Graham** – model reinventing our ideas of positive body image. **Lizzo** – singer and actor who gently weaponizes her points of difference and refuses to be shamed for existing. **Gary Vaynerchuk** – entrepreneur and influencer with endless energy and enthusiasm for pushing counter-intuitive ideas. **Motsi Mabuse** – dancer and *Strictly Come Dancing* judge who wears her emotions openly and combines vulnerability and extroversion in equal measure.

Chapter 6

BE LIKE A MAVERICK (LIKE CYNT)

HONE YOUR DANCE MOVES – AND DON'T SIT IN THE ASSIGNED SEAT

'What If . . .?' Happy High Status: Creative Optimism

Give yourself permission to do the thing

Cynthia Marshall, known as Cynt, was the first Black female CEO in the US's National Basketball Association. She was appointed to lead the Dallas Mavericks in 2018 after thirty-six years working in executive roles at the telecommunications company AT&T, where she specialized in improving workplace culture. In her autobiography *You've Been Chosen*, she talks about not waiting for anyone else to choose you and give you permission. She explains that you are already chosen. (In her world, by God. But I'm pretty sure you can also choose yourself. The point is, however you are chosen, you are already chosen.) This is a key happy high status message that I define as 'What if . . .?' energy. It's an extension of a sort of generosity and magnanimity: be open-minded, be open-hearted and also be open to possibility, to creating something that hasn't been seen before, to inhabiting a role in a way it hasn't been inhabited before. The confidence to do something need not be dependent on historical precedent, previous experience or external permission. You may have to be the first one. You may have to be the only one. You may have to ignore others who say it should be done a different way. You may have to do it before you are ready. But whatever the case, when you're 'What if . . .?' happy high status, you can afford to nod and smile, and do it your own way.

Known as 'Cynt the Sprint' from her running days at school, in her early career Marshall was told to change her hair and wear 'white clothes'. (Not meaning white in colour. Meaning 'like white people wear'. I dread to think what this was supposed to mean. It makes wearing a man's jacket in the boardroom seem normal.) She was told to use the name Cynthia instead of the name she had always gone by, Cynt. Or to maybe even change her name to Cindy as it 'sounded better'. (Also: what?!) She was told her voice was too loud and that she shouldn't maintain an 'open door' policy at work. She did not listen to any of this advice. Instead, she muddled through. She was optimistic and creative and she embraced 'What if . . .?' happy high status: '*What if I do things my way?*' '*What if I try something different?*' '*What if I ignore received wisdom?*'

It pays to practise and rehearse the habit of ignoring other people's (bad) advice and doing your own thing as early on in life and as often as you can. Cynt Marshall had been doing all this since her teens. She was the first African American president at her school and the first African American cheerleader at the University of California, Berkeley. She is often referred to as a 'maverick' but prefers to say that she just tells it like it is and doesn't mess about. 'Maverick' energy can feel off-putting to some people: experimentation and counter-intuitive thinking are essential for creatives and independents, but it can be dangerous to be a maverick in many professional environments, especially in a management or leadership role. But if you can import that spirit of disruption and originality in an empathetic and sensitive way into corporate life, it can be incredibly effective. Obviously, this is about being judicious and knowing your industry. In some fields you will stand out in a bad way if you are too much of a disruptor. In other fields, you will be invisible and irrelevant if you never try anything new or risky. No one wants a maverick accountant. (Except perhaps some politicians or oligarchs. And dodgy high status is not what we are aiming for here.)

In the right environment and with the right boundaries, mavericks are also usually able to get away with being more candid than most people. During her working life, Cynt has spoken openly about infertility, about having four miscarriages and about her premature baby daughter who died at the age of six months. She has not hesitated to share the story of her recovery from stage-three colon cancer when she was in her early fifties. She has done all this while pioneering straightforward ideas in business organization. As a human resources manager she has spearheaded the case for gender-neutral toilets since the early 1980s. She made it her duty to get people to support solutions ('What if . . .?'), rather than argue about the issue. Her philosophy is simple: treat people like humans; try to understand people and meet them where they are; find out who people are and why they're doing their job. Simplicity is a fantastic hallmark of happy high status. As Cynt puts it herself: 'Listen. Lead. Love.' (OK, I get that not everyone is ready for the last bit. But it can't hurt.)

Cynt's take on inclusion is a useful one and goes hand in hand with happy high status. She says it's not just about inviting people to the party but 'asking them to dance and accepting the dance moves that they bring'. Happy high status is not simply about how you behave in relation to yourself. It is also about what you can do for others. This attitude evolves into a virtuous circle: the more optimistic and less judgemental you are with others, the more compassionate and open you can be with yourself. Cynt's dance invitation is a great principle to bear in mind for our interactions with other people. But it's also a great principle to apply to yourself. Let yourself dance and bring your own moves. Don't be judging your dance moves any more than you would judge anyone else's.

Give up waiting to be confident – it's too long a wait

I do worry about people who are scared of their own dance moves. I see a lot of people second-guessing themselves, avoiding scrutiny, keeping their head beneath the parapet. The only 'What if . . .?' they embrace is: 'What if it's a better idea to stay under the duvet?' I'm not criticizing, because we all have days like that. And they can feel insurmountable when it seems as if everyone else is making great strides. Career profiles like Cynt Marshall's are striking simply because they are so extreme and eye-catching. She was 'the first' in almost every leadership role she occupied and she has made it her business to put openness and honesty at the heart of her story. These aren't things everyone is capable of. And I sometimes wonder whether the inspirational aspect of these stories might have an unintended counter-effect, and actually intimidate people. Do these stories unconsciously plant a negative thought? 'I'm not the first, so what does it matter?' Or: 'I definitely don't want to be the first.' Or: 'I'm glad someone is talking about those things openly but I wouldn't be comfortable doing that.'

These are all legitimate responses and we all have different paths. But one thing I have noticed on a much smaller scale, away from these electric, headline-grabbing 'firsts', is that people can often be afraid to be bold *in any way whatsoever* at work, let alone have the fantastically transformative energy of someone like Cynt Marshall. Some people are hiding away to such an extent that it's career-damaging. You don't have to be 'the first' and sign up to do a TED talk. You can influence things in a quiet way that is bold without having to be spectacular. There is a safe way to unleash your dance moves. One underrated way to be discreetly happy high status is to be quietly optimistic and dip a toe in the 'What if . . .?' water. You don't have to ask: 'What if I become the first woman to acquire a £500 billion share portfolio?' You can ask: 'What if I ask my colleague Alan out for coffee?' We rarely discuss the small but significant moves that require just the teeniest amount of courage. But these moves are also happy high status. And yet we resist these tiny leaps of faith.

I was at an event recently for a women's network in a big City company in London. A group of colleagues was gathering for the first time post-pandemic, and it was a big deal for company morale and for networking possibilities. As soon as I walked through the door and observed the way people were sitting, I could see that they were completely underwhelmed and exhausted. They weren't hostile, and they wanted to be there, but they clearly had very little, if any, surplus energy. It was not a 'Cynt the Sprint' vibe. During the Q&A, a sense of their state of mind started to emerge. The group was in the grip of a curious kind of timidity and caution. It took a while for them to talk about what was bothering them. Most of the questions were about how to ask for support from other women and how to ask for information and for mentoring from senior people. There was a general consensus that it was difficult, embarrassing, 'excruciating' to ask for help or advice. Someone said that in order to get a mentor or voice a problem you had to be confident, even extremely confident. They thought you had to be the type of person who wasn't scared of being the first, of standing out. Basically, not scared of being a Cynt.

Slowly, others admitted that they had also felt this way, but eventually, when they did get around to asking for advice, the reaction was always positive. The feeling of embarrassment and difficulty came not from what they experienced, it came from assumption and fear: 'I suddenly realized, "Oh, these are my colleagues and they don't think it's weird if I ask them if we can go for coffee."' Before this (very basic) realization, they were waiting to become more confident or waiting for someone to give them permission or some kind of guarantee. Some people waste years waiting to feel a certain way or waiting for something not to seem scary. And then it turns out that the awkwardness they were worried about was purely in their imagination.

This is what is fascinating: we champion tales of the Cynts, of 'firsts' and of breaking glass ceilings and 'smashing it'. Whatever that is. But in real life most people are scared to ask someone more senior than them out for coffee in case . . . Well, in case what? In case that person says: 'Who do you think you are to ask me for advice? I am a very busy person.' Or: 'I am going to report you for not being sufficiently committed to your role. Clearly you want a promotion. Who do you think you are?' No one says these things. And if they did, well, it's a good story about what a twit they are.

At this post-pandemic event, this phenomenon was reported even by the women who eventually did ask senior managers out for coffee to ask perfectly reasonable questions like, 'How do you make partner?' Or: 'What do I do if my manager is always ignoring my suggestions?' Women who had been there for ten years or more talked about how they looked back on their younger selves and wished that they had understood it was perfectly acceptable to ask someone more senior or from another department for advice. Instead they had waited to 'feel more confident'. Eventually, after a few more years, they weren't necessarily more confident but they were more impatient and they were done waiting. They realized that unless they started having these conversations they would have to leave the company anyway.

These conversations – the ones they had been working up the confidence to have – needed to take place or they would be replaced by similarly stressful conversations, requiring a lot of confidence, with headhunters or senior managers at other companies or, at the very least, with a career coach. Another common realization was that once you needed to negotiate maternity leave, it didn't matter whether you felt confident or not, you had no choice but to broach the subject and sort out the arrangements. The ones with children were the ones who had miraculously found a way to start speaking up for themselves without waiting for the mysterious mantle of confidence to land upon them out of the blue. The more you ask, the more you dare, the more you experiment, the stronger your happy high status. Don't wait to feel it. It is already there anyway, waiting to be used. There's a saying in French: 'L'appétit vient en mangeant.' It translates as: 'Appetite comes with eating.' The confidence equivalent? Confidence comes with doing, with asking, with not assuming, with going before you are ready. Not with waiting.

Being bold enough to risk rejecting your assigned seat

Some of this is about the – sometimes justified – fear of being seen to be a rule-breaker. Certainly, it is unsafe in many working cultures to be the maverick who asks, 'What if . . .?' But this fear also gets used as an excuse. I hear so many people saying that they 'can't' challenge certain norms at work or they 'can't' ask not to use slides ('because everybody uses slides') or they 'can't' ask for meetings to be a useful fifteen minutes instead of a useless hour. Confidence also becomes the scapegoat in these situations: 'These are things only a confident person would ask for and I'm not confident.' 'I'm not senior enough to ask that.' 'I have no idea how they might react.'

The latter is the key phrase here. Of course you have no idea how they might react, just as the women at the event I went to had no idea how their coffee invite would be received. (Actually very positively.) The worst thing that can happen is that you open a conversation. After that, see what happens. You're not seeking to control everything or throw a strop if your idea doesn't get taken up. So what if someone thinks you're overreaching or rocking the boat, or doing something that no one has ever tried to do before . . . Who cares? Maybe it works or maybe it doesn't. Either way you will learn something. This is one of the most basic and useful applications of fledgling, growing confidence: practising opening gambits, risking an intro-duction, creating some kind of opening for yourself. Yes, it takes happy high status to feel comfortable doing those things. But the more you do them, the easier it will come, the stronger the feelings of 'What if . . .?' happy high status.

The psychotherapist Esther Perel, known for her work on human behaviour, talks about this when she says: 'I never sit in my assigned seat.' It's her habit, in any situation, to decide last-minute where she is going to sit: at events, at the theatre. If she has a ticketed seat, she will look around to see if there is a better seat. It's the definition of creating an opening for yourself, forcing an opportunity: creativity, optimism. It is a really interesting test of 'What if . . .?' happy high status. You could argue that a truly confident person is really not going to be bothered what seat they're sitting in. They will make the best of whatever seat they have. They will not look for the 'best' seat. You could also seek to disrupt and then go with the flow: see where you end up – make the most of that. The consequence of this stance is interesting. If you take the risk to 'never sit in your assigned seat', you are voluntarily opening yourself up to circumstances you can't control and therefore also to potential conflict – and, provided you are not a psychopath, you are trusting yourself to resolve that conflict. That demonstrates a very enviable belief in yourself.

Why do I mention psychopaths? Because a person who never sits in their assigned seat, who expects everyone else to fall in around them, who will pick a fight and insist that a seat is theirs when they know it is not: that person is at least a sociopath, if not a psychopath. It's this extreme that we fear when we make requests and disrupt things. (See the 'wiseguys' of Chapter 3.) What if we've overstepped that social boundary? Will people think badly of us? Is this a mark of confidence or of arrogance? I can't imagine that Esther Perel is a sociopath, as everything I know about her behaviour from watching her interviews, and her online presence is that she is a gentle, kind and empathetic person who thinks about other people before she does things. Indeed, she has made a career out of reaching out to other people and trying to make their lives easier. Which is why this example really fascinated me: this is the one part of her life where she allows herself to be potentially 'selfish' (by taking the risk of occupying 'someone else's seat') and by doing something that constitutes 'breaking a rule'.

Perel describes waiting until the last moment to find a seat that she prefers (so that she doesn't risk taking anyone else's seat) and sometimes moving at the end of the first act to a better seat. (Full disclosure: I have also done this. If you're not coming by the end of the first act, you're not coming. You snooze, you lose, my friend.) In every instance 'not sitting in the assigned seat' means that you are taking a risk. Someone can come up to you and say, 'Sorry, I wanted that seat.' (The adult equivalent of 'I saw it first.') Other people could be inconvenienced by you taking up a seat at the last minute. The 'true' owner of the seat could emerge. But if you're happy high status, you know that if there is a challenge or there is a problem or there is an argument, you've got this. You can always laugh and say, 'I never sit in my assigned seat but I guess today is not my day.' The crucial difference as well is that you have an assigned seat. You have a back-up. So you can afford to try to upgrade it. This is a very small, manageable way of channelling that Cynt 'maverick' energy.

Of course, this is a particular example because if we all broke the rule of the assigned seat, no theatre show would start on time and there would be utter chaos as everyone would be waiting for everyone else to sit down. Society only runs effectively when most of us sit in our assigned seats most of the time. We don't want to cause anarchy. Not *everything* needs switching up. But what if we occasionally thought to ourselves, 'I don't always sit in my assigned seat . . .'? By this I mean that we could learn to think differently – and with true trust in ourselves to resolve the outcome using happy high status: 'I don't always do what is expected of me.' 'Sometimes I behave unpredictably.' 'Sometimes I surprise myself.' 'There are times when I do what I want to do instead of what others want me to do.' 'Sometimes I don't know how I'm going to behave.' 'Sometimes I wait until the last minute to see if there's a better option.' 'Sometimes I change my mind halfway through.' What difference would it make if we all trusted ourselves – from time to time, not all the time – to break out from our assigned seat and deal with the fallout from that?

In my imagination Esther Perel's experiment sometimes leads to great results. You get the best seat in the house, it wasn't sold anyway, no one challenges you and it's wonderful. Or – also not a bad result – you have a brief exchange with someone who, it turns out, did buy a ticket for that seat, you laugh about your attempt to steal their seat and they buy you a drink in the bar at the interval. (OK, I am always thinking about George Clooney and about people bringing me drinks that I didn't order. I admit it. Rumbled.) Worst-case scenario: you get to annoy a pompous or rule-bound person ever so slightly, a person who by the end of the first act will be enjoying their amazing seat so much that they will have completely forgotten who you are. What I'm wondering about here is an abstract extension of this principle. What if . . . we broke out from our assigned seats in all areas of life?

The 'safe maverick' version of caring less about what others think

When we can't ask 'What if . . .?', it can be because we are stuck within the thinking of a certain group or within certain boundaries that appear 'safe' or 'fixed'. The instinct to do the right thing by the group is sometimes called 'the social editor' (because we are editing our thoughts and our behaviour and selecting them according to what is socially acceptable) or 'the social filter'. (Hence the expression 'She's got no filter.') If you struggle with confidence, it's worth asking if your social filter is overdeveloped or too cautious. How can you push that boundary very slightly without feeling exposed? It's understandable why we might not do this often, as we all learn as children: 'Do as you're told or you will suffer the consequences.' Sometimes obedience is necessary, and as we've explored already in Chapter 4, we observe many spoken and unspoken rules in life in order to preserve civility and avoid conflict. Of course, not everyone can sit in the best seats in the theatre. For those of us who would like to feel more confident and who dream of having more Cynt-like moments, there is often a deep mistrust of any instinct that feels maverick or renegade. It can feel safer to be sensible, to be invisible, to stay under the radar. The more you think like that, the more you are likely to find yourself harbouring negative feelings towards anyone who does the opposite. You might even think of them as 'show-offs', 'big-mouths' or 'self-promoters'. You really care about making sure no one ever thinks that about you.

Clearly some people need more, not less, self-awareness just as some people could afford to be a little less sure of their own confidence. But that is their problem. The issue with people who want to be *more* confident is that they fear – intensely – being mistaken for being overconfident. So they go to the complete-opposite extreme in order to avoid that perception and instead adopt a position of under-confidence. We become afraid of heading towards the seat that has not been assigned to us in case someone says, 'Well, that's very cheeky and rude. You are a hideous, arrogant person.' We might even go so far as to imagine that they might hit us in the face. If you pull that extreme right back and consider the opposite, generous response, the other person might say: 'No problem, easy mistake to make.' Or: 'Do you know what? I don't want to sit here anyway. Let's swap.'

We very easily catastrophize and expect the worst – a natural but self-defeating reaction that reflects some kind of self-protection or a deflection of an anticipated slight. Many people will go to any lengths to avoid being challenged on their confidence. This is why when you talk to them about public speaking, they will say that they don't want to stand up straight, take pauses and look the audience in the eye because they are afraid that the audience 'will think that I'm full of myself'. Well, no, they probably won't. They will probably be a) thinking about what they're going to have for tea, and b) grateful that someone is actually talking to them instead of reading from boring notes. Other people are rarely thinking the terrible things that we fear they are thinking. (And even if they are, so what? Do you really think you can stop them? Do you really think it matters?) Trying to deflect criticism that may never actually materialize and is probably in your own head anyway is one of the worst reasons to stay unconfident. Although it's a very successful method for staying unconfident. So if you want to remain terrified of your own shadow, then keep on focusing on that non-existent anticipated criticism.

The antidote to this is optimistic creativity. So how, in practical terms, do you embrace the spirit of Cynt and be a 'safe maverick'? Small, manageable experiments and challenges that push you just out of your comfort zone. Open conversations with trusted friends and colleagues about your strengths and about the areas in your life where you could afford to take more risks. Easy, repeatable actions that build up to a picture that can be measured over time. (For example, committing to regular posts if you have decided to be more visible on social media.) Ridiculously simple, as Cynt puts it: 'The secret to getting things done is to act.' Committing to small actions gives you a history of evidence: what worked, what didn't. That evidence gives you proof of competence and competence grows confidence. Confidence gives you the conviction to know what is 'too maverick' and what is 'just maverick enough' in your field of influence. And all the time, without even realizing it, you will also be increasing your 'What if . . . ?' happy high status.

How to get a piece of it

• This thought is useful: 'What if I didn't think that [negative thing] about myself to quite that extent?' Start to think about the stories you tell yourself about why you don't feel confident in certain situations, about why you say no to particular opportunities or about long-held fears that you'd like to let go of. Write down these justifications and beliefs. (Sometimes called 'limiting beliefs'.) So you would write something like: 'I hate public speaking because

I always think I'm going to forget what I was going to say.' Or: 'I'm not the best person in my team to appear on a panel because I don't have enough gravitas.' Or: 'I'm just shy, really, so I don't want to stand up in front of other people.' Dig deep and mine as many of these statements as you can. What if these statements are not 100 per cent true? What if you tweaked them? Instead of 'I hate public speaking', put 'I used to hate public speaking.' Or: 'I hate public speaking *in certain situations.*' It's hard to hold on to a fear once we stop generalizing. Ask: 'What if I toned down that negative belief a little? What emerges?'

- Learn to live with fear of error (Part One). That fear of being 'too maverick' or of not knowing where to start when it comes to making a change, whether small or big, cannot be fixed by analysis. It requires trial and error. It's easier to embrace 'trial and error' if you commit to a process. Build into your process challenges that you can objectively meet so that your 'wins' are based on completion. For example, this is the difference between 'delivering a brilliant speech' (completely subjective) and 'spending sixty minutes a day working on the speech for the whole of this week, timed using my phone timer' (easy to tick off). Obviously, in meeting the 'timer' challenge you are more likely to deliver a brilliant speech anyway. But the point is, your confidence comes from the act of keeping your promise to yourself and through the enjoyment of the work itself. Once that confidence starts growing and you're taking on more 'trials' (or 'experiments' or 'moments of trying out new things'), the 'error' part simply becomes the tweaks or lessons learned.

- Learn to live with fear of error (Part Two). Creative, open, maverick high status is the celebration of things going wrong. In improv comedy this is summed up by the phrase: 'We suck and we love to fail.' See also: 'What if it doesn't matter if you suck?' Once you get more comfortable with error, you can turn it to your advantage, make it part of your story. If you can find a way to explain the story of a loss or narrate something that went badly wrong, these things go down very well on social media. 'Don't make the same mistake I made. Here, let me tell you about it in great detail.' No one ever turns away from listening to that, especially if it comes from someone in the same industry. First, it can be engaging, compelling and inspiring to listen to these stories. Second, it's useful as we could all do with learning from other people's mistakes. Does admitting failure compromise the drive to be happy high status? No, not as long as you steer away from 'poor me' and think about how what you've learned relates to others, rather than wallowing in how tough it was for you. (That sounds harsh. Sorry. But you know what I mean.)

Inspiration for 'What if . . .?' happy high status: creative optimism

Traits: Relishes challenges and the idea that something hasn't been done before. Has multiple interests and passions and is interested in borrowing from all of them to find solutions. Brings qualities more commonly seen in one field into another (e.g. bringing the polish of showbusiness into politics or importing the compassion of the caring industries into sport).

Most useful for: Anyone facing a situation described as 'impossible'. Those facing leadership or creative roles where they are having to attempt something that hasn't been tried before. Anyone with a point to prove or an idea they want to experiment with.

Who succeeds at this: **Alexandria Ocasio-Cortez** – politician and activist who combines glamour, intellectual rigour and approachability in a political role. **Es Devlin** – artist and stage designer known for 'outside the box' thinking and a can-do attitude resulting in never-seen-before installations in huge spaces. **Paula Kahumbu** – charismatic conservationist and broadcaster who combines practical activism with public education. **Amanda Gorman** – poet and campaigner who spoke at President Biden's inauguration, known for quiet intellectual strength and calm self-possession. **Andrea Gibson** – poet and activist who has extraordinary intensity, powerful sensitivity and a ton of self-deprecating humour in their public performances and viral videos.

Chapter 7

BE LIKE A DANCING POLITICIAN

IDIOSYNCRASY, ORIGINALITY IN LEADERSHIP AND BEING 'HIGH ON THE PEAR'

'Leader' Happy High Status:
Redefining Authority

'I just want to be honest and be myself. I find it much easier.' – Sanna Marin

Are there limits to that joyous, maverick creativity? Maybe it's only appropriate in certain circumstances? Can you be creative, optimistic, open and still maintain authority? Don't you have to play it safe if you want to be a leader? Well, let's see. In late August 2022, during the period of high summer known in good old-fashioned Fleet Street journalism as 'the silly season' (because there isn't much happening and 'silly' stories are more likely to get reported), the name Sanna Marin made headlines across the globe. Sanna Marin's name ought really to have already been better known outside of her homeland at the time, even to those who don't watch politics closely. She became the youngest prime minister in the world (and youngest female head of state) when, at the age of thirty-four in 2019, she was sworn into office in Finland. At the time, she headed up a five-party coalition in which every leader was female and under forty, a fact which attracted excitement and curiosity, including at that year's Davos World Economic Forum, where she was asked how on earth 'a government like that' functioned. 'Like any government,' she responded.

Marin is well known in Finland for her expert management of coalition politics and first sprang to fame at home thanks to a viral video of a debate about a high-speed tram where she exhibited common sense and nerves of steel while chairing an interminable ten-hour meeting. She also happens to be a great case study for calm, introverted speakers: her addresses are measured and the definition of sensible. Like a lot of European leaders, she's made some great speeches in English. Overall, she's a sensible, measured, intellectual sort of person. Not a maverick. Maybe even a bit boring. Which, for a politician, I mean as the ultimate compliment.

During the summer of 2022, though, it was another viral video that made her notorious, a video far more exciting than the one deliberating the traffic infrastructure of southern Finland. In mid-August, video footage of Marin singing, dancing and drinking wine at a party with friends was leaked. It caught the imagination of editors and commentators around the world, as well as drawing praise from anyone who has ever let their hair down after a tough week. The response was immediately divided. Some seemed to suggest that this behaviour was scandalous and unbecoming of a senior politician. Additional footage showed guests at the party exhibiting even more 'raucous' behaviour, possibly under the influence of drugs. The provenance of the video was investigated and analysed. The leak had likely come via a friend or an acquaintance, leading to the conclusion that even if you didn't mind Sanna Marin's behaviour, you probably agreed that she should at least be more discerning about who she lets into the circle of trust. Some laid into her and insisted this was a display of arrogance and entitlement. But many argued that this was not a show of 'too much confidence' or some kind of betrayal of the status of her office. It was simply an inevitability of twenty-first-century life. Marin was just 'being herself'. Is this 'leader' happy high status and a redefinition of the parameters of authority? Or is it a scene from Satan's waiting room?

Marin undertook a drugs test and released a statement that she did not take drugs, that she had been drinking 'moderately' and had been at her desk working first thing the next morning. Her supporters felt that she didn't need to explain herself at all. Thousands of online videos – mostly of enviably attractive middle-aged Scandinavian women rocking out at parties holding glasses of wine – floodedsocialmediaunderthehashtag#solidaritywithsanna. Hillary Clinton signalled her support by posting a picture of herself on the dance floor: 'As Ann Richards said, "Ginger Rogers did everything that Fred Astaire did. She just did it backwards and in high heels." Here's me in Cartagena while I was there for a meeting as Secretary of State. Keep dancing, Sanna Marin.' (Intended message: secretaries of state can also get down.) In short: this video was a litmus test. How much confidence is too much? Is it OK to be truly relaxed and confident in public or only in private? Does it mean people stop taking you seriously, especially as a woman? Or is even asking that question old-fashioned and patriarchal? This is a conundrum when thinking about the parameters for your own 'leader' happy high status. It demonstrates an issue many people have with confidence: we can't always work out whether certain behaviours are aspirational or even appropriate because we don't have consensus.

The court of your own conscience

So what was going on here? Is Sanna Marin – or any other partying politician – happy high status because she's behaving like a normal person? Or is it her job to demonstrate a special kind of 'leader' happy high status by avoiding the things that normal people do? As a planet, we don't have a lot of experience of witnessing young female leaders who like drinking wine and dancing with their friends at the weekend. Sadly, Margaret Thatcher and Angela Merkel did not do much of the groundwork in this department. But just because we haven't seen something before or it's new to us, doesn't mean that it's wrong. This is about changing norms – and about the expansion of our understanding of what authority is. For some people this behaviour represented the ultimate in 'leader' happy high status. Here was a perfectly normal, confident, happy 36-year-old woman having a good time with her friends, enjoying a life outside work, letting her hair down without letting it affect her professionalism or her seriousness. For others, though, this was not any kind of happy high status.

This was barbarism. How can anyone take a woman seriously once it emerges that she has friends, goes to parties and likes dancing? (Yes, I did write that in a Jane Austen voice.)

This example doesn't seem immediately relevant to our own everyday quest to work out our individual version of 'leader' happy high status. But this is not about the fact of the behaviour itself or the ubiquity of phone cameras and social media in the lives of senior politicians. This is about judgement and what we consider 'safe', especially in a professional context. How do we know when we are 'too much'? If you push the boundaries of informality and 'relaxed' leadership, or you allow yourself to be vulnerable, or you speak up passionately in an environment where people aren't usually passionate ... How can you know that won't backfire on you? How do you know when you are 'just being yourself'? Or when you have gone too far?

The polarized reaction to Sanna Marin's dance party is the perfect example of changing and unpredictable societal expectations. For starters, a norm is being challenged: someone who is young, a woman, in an informal situation, an attractive human being who looks like a movie star and not a boring politician, is in power. But it is also an irresistibly powerful water cooler moment in the sense that the existence of the video itself becomes a talking point. Who took this footage? Why did they release it? What are other people saying about it? It demonstrates why a lot of people do feel cautious and uncertain, and spend their lives waiting for someone else to give them permission. When a norm is challenged, it raises questions. It's a reminder of the Elbert Hubbard quote: 'To escape criticism: say nothing, do nothing, be nothing.' There are echoes here too of a favourite Jacinda Ardern quote of mine: 'If you sit and wait to feel like you are the most confident person in the room, you are probably going to be left by yourself.' In other words: you have to take a leap of faith to feel truly confident.

An additional dimension to this fear of criticism is that we worry about overstepping some boundary that we might not even know about. We're perhaps more likely to harbour that anxiety now, compared with a hundred years ago, as societal norms are no longer as clear and fixed as they used to be, especially for people who are occupying positions in society that they wouldn't have occupied before. We don't know whether they should be allowed to be confident in this behaviour, because it has not been previously displayed. The boundaries of 'leader' happy high status are not fixed. And that is liberating. But also daunting.

This plays out in day-to-day office politics as well as on the international stage. I have come up against this with senior women who want to use certain language and gestures in speeches or meetings. For example, they might want to use a speech to lay out a vision for their department or for the future of the company, but there is no precedent for a woman – or maybe for anyone – taking that initiative and so they can't work out whether to do so would be bold and praiseworthy, or risky and foolhardy.

How do you make a 'leader' happy high status decision in that situation? I would always argue that you may as well err on the side of risk and trust yourself to find a way to row back if it lands badly. Because if you don't risk anything, nothing changes. But I also recognize that it depends on the conservatism of a company's culture and on your personal standing at a given moment. The trouble is, you often find yourself in situations where there is no one who can tell you the right thing to do and where the only opinion you can lean on is your own. This example is simply proof of 'the court of your own conscience': the ability to trust your own judgement about what sits right with you. Sylvia Plath used this expression to judge whether her writing was any good or not: she meant it as an acknowledgement that ultimately the only person who can give you meaningful approval is yourself. When you exude authority and you have understood what that looks like on you and what that feels like for you, you no longer second-guess yourself. 'Leader' happy high status individuals trust their own judgement deeply and implicitly. Which in turn has the knock-on effect of inspiring trust in others.

Having the guts to be the changing face of leadership

Sanna Marin has no real case to answer here. And her own judgement will have told her that. But it's also obvious that there's a double standard at work. How is her behaviour really any different from, or more scandalous than, that of, say, Winston Churchill? Yes, it's him again. I like bringing him up as an example because he's such an extreme personality type – and one very much of his time – and yet he is still frequently cited as a source for inspirational leadership. He called his morning whisky 'mouthwash', and drank brandy and champagne at lunch. His lifetime consumption was once estimated at 42,000 bottles of Pol Roger champagne. If we are talking about personal milestones, forget leading your country. This is truly a world-beating achievement. Kind of makes you want to revisit But-I'm-Not-Winston-Churchill syndrome. If we had access to a video of the epic drinking sessions he had with Franklin D. Roosevelt – who used to need ten-hour 'naps' after spending time with the British premier – would we be lauding this as a fantastically 'confident' way to lead? Or would we think it looked a bit tragic and patrician? The point is, Churchill's habits and proclivities were well known: he slept for two hours every afternoon, which he said allowed him to complete one and a half days' work in twenty-four hours. No drug or alcohol tests for him. No questions about his commitment to the job. Instead, his behaviour and mindset are written up in business books about maximum efficiency and the authenticity of genius.

I'm not trying to argue here that Winston Churchill or Sanna Marin are 'right' or 'wrong'. Politicians can do what they like and others can vote for them or not. But I want to point out that our perception of what is permissible in high office – or at any level of leadership – changes radically throughout history, and depends on the person exercising that behaviour. What is seen as 'confident' or 'exuberant' changes over time and according to who is judging it. It's nearly seventy years since Churchill was in power but I cannot imagine it being possible for any woman anywhere in the world to be able to hold political office while having a known and publicized lifetime consumption of 42,000 bottles of champagne. (But if it does become possible, I am open to sponsorship opportunities.) There may equally have been a similar hesitation to accept this from a younger male politician, too, at any point in time. Churchill was in his late sixties when he took office as prime minister, so perhaps there was an attitude that if he had got away with living like this for so long, then how bad can it be?

The point is that we allow licence and leeway to people who conform to what we already think of as 'leaders'. Which is why Churchill gets away with it – and is even enhanced by some kind of reputation as a 'genius' not subject to the vagaries of normal mortal life. ('He's just not like the rest of us.' I am waiting for this standard to be applied to an eccentric and florid female leader.) Sanna Marin, at first glance, does not get that free pass. But our minds are changing, slowly. Ultimately, the rosé-fuelled hashtag brigade – #solidaritywithsanna – won out in this instance, collectively making the case for a changing face of leadership: authenticity, normality, informality, fun, imperfection.

If I sound like I am trying to have it both ways here,

then you're right. I'm doing that on purpose. This is not about saying, 'It's perfectly acceptable to be the 36-year-old prime minister of a country and be videoed partying all night.' For some voters, yes, this might make her more attractive and 'real' to them. I, personally, certainly don't blame her for letting her hair down. For others, it will be a step too far either because they disapprove or because they think as a public figure it's distracting from your job to draw attention to yourself. If she were my prime minister and it had been in the middle of a pandemic, I would have felt differently about it. We do have different standards for people in high office and it's only in the past few decades that we are seeing different kinds of people in those offices, so it's not surprising when there is no consensus over an incident like this.

Whether 'right' or 'wrong', it's still an important example to consider, and one that is not really just about what is acceptable behaviour for a politician. It goes to the heart of our changing views on public versus private, what constitutes authenticity, what constitutes leadership, how confident is 'too confident' and whether we are ready to see certain people in certain roles. The key thing is that all of us need to feel comfortable in our own behaviour and know that we approve of ourselves. In this sense both Churchill and Marin are 'right' because – it seems to me – they were both comfortable with their choices and could look themselves in the eye. This is true confidence, even if others haven't quite caught up with you yet. After all, it doesn't really matter how anyone else judges you if you have put the time and the consideration into your attitude and your behaviour. To be able to say, 'I stand by my dancing.' *That* is 'leader' happy high status.

'What's she got to be so confident about?'

Resistance to fresh or unfamiliar expressions of leadership is just another variation on that old chestnut, 'How is she getting away with that?' Or: 'Who does she think she is?' (Gender-neutral equivalent: 'The new CEO is *how old*? I have underwear older than that.') It's a way of expressing unease about the changes we are seeing in society without saying, 'I'm really not sure I'm comfortable with a 36-year-old woman leading this country.' Or: 'I want all leaders to look the same as they did a hundred years ago because I don't like change.' It's not socially acceptable to say those words, so people find another way to get that message across. Questioning someone's confidence in what they are doing – and whether we should still have confidence in them – is a very easy way to do that. There will always be a counterpoint or a raised eyebrow. It doesn't matter how confident we become – or even how well we manage to handle a difficult or awkward question – we can always be subject to challenges to our confidence. There will always be someone who wants to say: 'Justify yourself. Explain why we should believe in you.'

A few months after the party-video storm, a challenge arose following a meeting between Sanna Marin and New Zealand's then prime minister, Jacinda Ardern. One floundering journalist asked if the two were meeting 'just because you're similar in age and have a lot of common stuff there . . .' 'Common stuff'? A very poor question by any standard. But the headlines reporting these bilateral trade talks were even more telling: 'Ardern and Marin dismiss claim they met due to "similar age".' This makes it sound as if there was a movement of people who had become suspicious about these two women meeting, as if they had got together to plan a joint birthday party or had just found out they were twin sisters separated at birth, instead of meeting to talk about trade between their two nations and about Finland's application to join NATO. These two leaders are actually five years apart in age, in any case. And there was never any real 'claim'. It was just a confidence challenge. Ardern replied: 'I wonder whether or not anyone ever asked Barack Obama and John Key if they met because they were a similar age.' She added: 'Because two women meet is not simply because of their gender.' Marin replied that they were meeting 'because we are prime ministers'. I'm surprised she didn't offer to draw him a diagram.

This is a pretty good example – and one that is not only applicable to female prime ministers in their late thirties and early forties – of how 'leader' happy high status is not a shield against the stupidity of others. It's gratifying perhaps that most of the coverage about this questioning pointed out that it was sexist. And it was. But it's also true that once you are doing anything interesting or worthwhile (and what's the point in doing anything else?), you will always encounter some form of opposition or someone who wants to tear it down. Building confidence offers some protection, as it gives you a sense of calm when this inevitably crops up. The more calmly you respond – as if you anticipated it, which I imagine Ardern and Marin would have done as they will have encountered this kind of questioning before ('You're a woman. And you're a prime minister. Isn't that weird?') – the more you reinforce your confidence. It's a virtuous circle. Anticipate opposition. Do not link your own confidence to random opinions. As marketing expert Seth Godin puts it: 'Shun the non-believers.'

Crossing the line to overconfidence

Aside from the avoidance of criticism, the other reason we fear exhibiting behaviours that are 'too much' is because we fear crossing over into showing off. There is a beautiful expression in Norwegian that means 'to be full of oneself', to be insufferably arrogant: 'He's high on the pear.' (*Høy på pæren.*) From what I can understand as a non-Norwegian speaker, it has the same kind of connotation as 'getting high on your own supply'. So it really means that you've overdone it, you've gone too far, you've over-stepped the mark. You believe the sun shines out of an unmentionable place. No one wants to be your friend. These expressions almost always carry within them a sort of punishment: 'Pride comes before a fall.' It's not simply that someone is arrogant. They are so arrogant that they will soon be brought down a peg. They are an accident waiting to happen. This is such a commonly held belief, no wonder it encourages people to not bother trying to be confident in the first place. The risks of going too far possibly outweigh the benefits. Don't get high on the pear, whatever you do!

As adults, people who have anxieties about their confidence usually go out of their way to make sure that other people don't think they are high on the pear. They will avoid public speaking completely, push anyone other than themselves into the spotlight and generally hide their light under a bushel. No risk of leaked viral videos for them! This reticence is understandable when we ridicule people who give themselves airs and graces. *Høy på pæren* is also the Norwegian name for the British TV sitcom *Keeping Up Appearances*, about Hyacinth Bucket ('It's pronounced "bouquet"'), a woman who is the patron saint of unconvincing, self-deluding overconfidence, forever trying to portray herself as 'better' than she is. Most people say that they want to be confident. Or even if they won't admit it for themselves, then they would probably say they'd want confidence for their children, for example. But no one – no one – wants to be Hyacinth Bucket. Better to hide away than risk that, right?

Where is the line, then, between foolishly conceited and inspiringly confident? There's a lot of hypocrisy around our desire for confidence and our supposed rejection of people who we consider to be 'too confident'. Seeing as confidence is supposed to be something that is lightly worn, effortless, authentic, breezy, we ironically betray our obsession by overanalysing it and quantifying it, even if we never come close to directly identifying exactly where the line lies. We can't work out why some people seem to cross it and be forgiven, and yet others cross it and never find a way back. I'm sorry to say, for any fans of his, that Donald Trump is the obvious illustration of this. For many people he is an example of preposterously overcooked confidence. He's not just high on the pear: he's bought the entire orchard, painted all the pears gold, then remortgaged it but still claims to be the sole owner. And yet. To many people (including tens of millions who voted for him) he represents genuine unassailable confidence and enviable self-belief. It would be wrong to say – however much you wanted to (and I do really want to) – that Donald Trump is *not* a good role model for confidence. Because clearly to many people he *is* that very thing, otherwise they wouldn't support him.

There are two lessons here. The first is that 'too much' is *always* going to be 'too much' for someone. And you simply cannot please everyone all the time. The only thing you can do is take your cue from yourself. And second, our evaluation of 'socially acceptable confidence' is not fixed anyway. It changes from year to year or decade to decade. Our standards of beauty change over time. Our tastes change over time. And what we get used to and what we expect is constantly evolving. Why wouldn't our definition of confidence also change?

What we regard as 'the acceptable level of self-belief' is

in a constant state of flux. This is both a good thing and a bad thing. It's good because it means there is room for experimentation and for us to see something we haven't seen before. But it's bad because it means that it's difficult to point to one particular mode of behaviour and say: 'Do it like this and you'll be fine.' Once again, we're reminded that the aim of this book is not to pinpoint some kind of 'do it like this' standard of confidence, but instead to do something much more ambitious: to imbue you with a sense of trust in your own abilities and judgement. Once you've established that, you will get a sense of what that standard looks like for you – both in yourself and when you see it in others. Ultimately, the kind of confidence you are looking for is a confidence that can withstand other people saying that you are 'too confident'. It is also a confidence that can weather failure, mistakes, stupidity, hubris, blind spots and all the other errors that make us human. Because, remember, the only court of conscience that you have to answer to is your own.

The key point about 'leader' happy high status is that it is not static or fixed. Of course there are always 'classic' lessons in leadership, rhetoric and self-presentation that are going to stand the test of time. Take the Greek principles of logos, ethos and pathos – using our speech to appeal to logic, to build trust and to evoke emotions. That is never going to go out of fashion. But I do wonder if many of our previous definitions of happy high status are going to crumble in the decades to come. I would argue that Winston Churchill, for example – a staple of public-speaking manuals for the past century – has long appeared to most modern readers as an archaic, remote example. The word 'relatable' is overused and really quite annoying, but 'relatable' Winston Churchill is not. Instead of being the gold standard of tone, force of personality and choice of words, I don't think it's unfair to suggest that to many contemporary students of power and speaking, he comes across as privileged, entitled, stuffy. Once upon a time, that version of confidence might have been enviable and aspirational. No longer. Better to study a slightly intro-verted young Finnish woman who likes listening to Rage Against the Machine. Even better to study your own strengths and put the thought and energy into the unique creation that is your own 'leader' happy high status.

How to get a piece of it

- 'Leader' happy high status is the variation perhaps most dependent on cast-iron self-evaluation. Be wary of basing your evaluation of yourself on the opinion of others, especially in a professional context. Outside of work, we can choose who we hang out with, so we can avoid people who make us feel 'less than'. In work, we will always encounter people we can't avoid who challenge us in some way. Someone will always reject or resent your leadership. That's life. You can be the most self-assured person in the world and someone will think you are 'not enough' or 'too much'. Do not be confident for them. Be confident for yourself.

- Be aware of your best qualities and of your shortcomings. Give yourself credit for things you do that others don't. Some leaders are great at listening and being encouraging, at giving others confidence. Others are great at seeing the bigger picture, analysing the fine detail or noticing pitfalls before they arise. No one is ever going to ask you to stop doing any of those things. Beware of discounting things that are second nature to you. There is too much focus on 'confidence' being about people who are loud or self-assured, or always able to have the last word. Our more subtle, less showy qualities are also 'confidence'. Let them shine.

- Be wary of people who are always giving feedback and have a judgement on everything. When you are developing your confidence, especially in leadership roles, treat criticism as sacred: be very careful what you listen to and what you act on. Naturally we should all be open to constructive criticism and there's a time and place for it. A rule I live by is: the same criticism from three or more trusted sources is something you need to pay attention to. We shouldn't resist change or avoid this kind of critical feedback, but there is a culture of intense, for-its-own-sake feedback in a lot of work environments now that is often problematic and unhelpful. An individual response is just that: individual. It is one person's opinion. Unless feedback is consistent, quantifiable and replicated (the 'at least three trusted sources' rule), it risks being meaningless. Many people give feedback, good and bad, because they like giving feedback. It doesn't make the feedback useful. One employee complained to me recently that in their company most of their colleagues are spending more time on giving and processing '360-degree feedback' than on their actual work. I can't gauge whether that is demonstrably true – perhaps it was a 'feedback avoidant' person who hates change that said this – but there's a helpful message in there. Too much feedback for its own sake is toxic. If ever you can't physically get away from unhelpful, overly critical people, then try to screen them out and tell yourself a different story while they're talking. ('I will practise looking engaged and interested while they bang on with yet another criticism.')

Inspiration for 'leader' happy high status: redefining authority

Traits: Classic achiever background, but not necessarily the profile of a person who would have held a leadership role fifty years ago. Cast-iron self-belief is worn lightly and combined with respect for others' beliefs, even when they are opponents. Serious about their task but able to experiment within their role.

Most useful for: Anyone in a leadership or authority role where no one like you has done that role before. More traditional leaders who want to loosen up and leave room for creativity. Anyone who feels their role makes them 'rigid' or having to pretend to be something they're not.

Who succeeds at this: **Maia Sandu** – President of Moldova, known for her anti-corruption stance. **Fiona Hill** – foreign affairs specialist who gave testimony at Trump's impeachment trial and who combines deep knowledge and straightforward self-expression. **Ngozi Okonjo-Iweala** – first woman and first African to lead the World Trade Organization, known for her pragmatism and realism. **Ketanji Brown Jackson** – an associate justice of the Supreme Court of the United States, famous for her forensic questioning and dubbed 'a force to be reckoned with'. **Francia Márquez** – Vice President of Colombia and social activist, who has a legendary openness and lightness of touch.

Chapter 8

BE LIKE A BENCHED FOOTBALLER

PUBLIC FAILURE, GRACE IN DEFEAT AND THE ROLE OF EGO

Athletic Happy High Status:
Suppressing Ego in Service
of Excellence

Happy high status is not about always being on the winning side

At the UEFA Women's Euro Final on Sunday, 31 July 2022, the most memorable images of the match – clips that were replayed over and over – were the jubilant faces of goal-scorers Ella Toone and Chloe Kelly as England were crowned champions following a dramatic extra-time victory. England had beaten Germany two nil, and these were inspirational scenes, witnessed by an ecstatic audience of 17 million, the highest viewing figures for any women's football match in UK television history. Although we are used to seeing solo women triumph at, say, Wimbledon, and occasionally we see female teams celebrating swimming, gymnastics or track wins at the Olympics, spectators don't often get to see what it looks like when a female team is triumphant, celebrating in the way that only a football team can celebrate. It just isn't part of the visual landscape we have grown up with. This was a landmark moment: for women's sport internationally; for how women athletes are regarded; for the prominence they are given ... It was nothing short of monumental to see women triumph at this level, when only fifty years earlier they were not allowed to compete. (Women's football was literally banned in England until 1971.) This was a powerful illustration of happy high status for women's football in all senses: thousands of memes and shareable images were generated and video clips of their moments of celebration were shared endlessly. As well as being an important moment in sporting and television history, it felt like a moment of cultural change.

And yet. Despite the tangible symbolism of this victory, it was the face of a woman crushed by defeat that I think is the most fascinating and instructive about the significance of the moment. The idea that confident leadership is fluid and infinite goes hand in hand with a reframing of 'the win'. Five minutes before kick-off, a woman who could have been a potential player of the match – and who was a favourite for the tournament's Golden Boot award – had been forced to withdraw after sustaining a muscular injury during the warm-up. Germany's 31-year-old Alexandra Popp, an Olympic gold medallist, had at the time scored 59 goals in 119 international matches. She had also scored a goal in every match at the 2022 Euros running up to that moment, despite having tested positive for Covid three weeks beforehand and despite having been dogged by injury for eleven months of the previous year and repeatedly during her career. It was her team's most important match and she wasn't even going to take part in it. The camera followed her briefly as she left the pitch, biting her lip and blowing her cheeks out, during what must have been one of the worst moments of her life. Instead of scoring against England, she sat that match out on the sidelines, later saying with trademark understatement: 'It's a little bit hard.' No tantrums, no swearing, no scowling. This is athletic happy high status: being honest about your failure but not over-dramatizing and making it about you.

What was reflected only tangentially at the time on the live coverage was the sight of the German team's defeat, first through the images of Alexandra Popp, excluded from play, and later for the team as a whole, dazed in the aftermath of the match and resigned during the closing ceremony. We don't think twice about the confidence of winners. But the face of a loser has something vital to teach us about flexible confidence, the elasticity of happy high status and how to maintain self-belief in moments that are, well, really unhappy. Just as we rarely see female teams celebrating in the dazzlingly Amazonian and warrior-like way England celebrated that day, we equally don't often get to see what it looks like when female teams *lose*. The year before, when the England men's team lost to Italy on penalties at Euro 2020, it was difficult not to watch open-mouthed and ashamed when most of the team refused to take their second-place ('loser') medals at the closing ceremony. Medal refusal does happen in football, of course, and it is not that uncommon. But it is truly an opposite-of-happy-high-status thing to witness. Yes, we get it: you're disappointed and you didn't want to lose. No one ever does. But what about the teams who are in third, fourth, tenth place? You beat them. At least celebrate that. The human instinct to define victory and defeat as polar opposites that have no place side-by-side on the same platform is extraordinarily powerful. But it is also incredibly foolish. Because the one does not exist without the other.

When it came to their turn, the German women's team portrayed a completely different picture of losing. Perhaps it is overstating it to say that their display in defeat was even more inspiring than England's win. But it still tells us a lot. Because when you win, it's not difficult to celebrate. When you lose, it's very difficult to maintain anything resembling happy high status. In a complete reversal of the England men's team's behaviour, at the women's final, Alexandra Popp was noble and respectful in her personal experience of exclusion and the German team – though obviously broken – kept their medals on. They were visibly gutted and torn apart by the loss, but they were entirely dignified in their defeat, metaphorically putting their hands up: 'You beat us.' They didn't pretend it was anything other than the disappointment it clearly was, and they didn't sugar-coat it. This is the kind of behaviour that is contagious. If one person in a team is gracious and respectful in defeat, everyone else follows. But if someone makes a display of supposedly patriotic, sporting disappointment by removing their medal, it's very hard for their teammates to show them up by keeping theirs on. (Not that this is ever going to be a personal dilemma for most of us, especially not me.) The high-risk environment of sport – where there is often a fine line between victory and defeat – illustrates a basic truth about athletic happy high status: it is not about 'winning'. It is about the suppression of ego in service of excellence.

Alexandra Popp had already set the standard here when she left the pitch during the warm-up. She wore the face of stoic disappointment, not wanting to spoil the match for her teammates when she was 'robbed of her fairy-tale ending', as headlines at the time put it. As a player on the pitch she is described as being 'an absolute machine', 'lethal' and 'intimidating'. But to those who play alongside her she is, according to her teammate Pia-Sophie Wolter, known for 'being open' and 'always joking around': 'When you are standing on the pitch with her, she is a player who lifts you up, keeps you going and is an absolute leader.' This is the kind of emotional range that we need to think about when we are considering happy high status: assertive, fierce and a force to be reckoned with at times – and yet also gentle, calm, graceful and sanguine when the moment demands it. Happy high status says: 'I can lead and I can follow. I am no better than others and I am no worse than others. I can win and I can lose.' I love Alexandra Popp's reaction to that day: completely sensitive, open and free of ego, giving credit to her team, which also means giving credit to her team's opponents. 'My muscle said, "No, it is not for you." I am sad about it. Also, I'm proud of the team. We had a great tournament.' How is that attitude not a win in itself?

Let go of the outcome

As I explained in the introduction, there are two sides to confidence: internal and external. These two sides of ourselves – the external projection experienced by others and the internal feelings known only to the self – are in constant dialogue with each other. The stagecraft ideas from comedy and theatre that contributed to the term happy high status are about the external projection of confidence which is visible to others. That's why it's useful to think about body language, the expression on your face, how you hold yourself and all that other actorly stuff. But the other side of it is purely internal: how you handle your own feelings and how you filter the messages you tell yourself. In sport, the second part – the mindset and psychology of confidence – is far more important than playing a 'role'. In sport, your body has other things to worry about. (Unless you are a dancer, a gymnast or a figure skater, and then you've got to worry about your internal *and* external expressions. This is why athletes often struggle with performance and facial expressions on TV shows like *Strictly Come Dancing* or *Dancing on Ice*. In most sports, it is permissible to show effort or strain on your face as you are trying to reach a physical goal. In dance and gymnastics, the effort must be camouflaged in order to enhance the beauty of the performance.)

Integrating the two parts that make up happy high status is not about 'winning' every time and coming out on top every time. The main internal work is about rewiring your attitude. Arguably our good old friend George is not 'winning' when he has to break up his evening to follow you across a crowded room carrying a drink. But he turns it into a win when he converts this potential (and only ever fictional, imaginary) loss of face, minor insult or petty humiliation into a chance for a moment of human connection, into an opportunity to show how human he is, into a smile and a laugh instead of a grimace and a punch. Athletic happy high status is about playing your own game. Or perhaps a better way of putting it is: instead of winning at life, it's about winning at being human. Which maybe is the same thing, but the expression 'winning at life' has pretty much come to mean 'getting one over on someone else' or 'having it better than anyone else' or 'having something that not everyone can have'. Athletic happy high status does not exclude others or push anything in their face.

We don't often see the 'happy loser' in public life and I have to wonder if that adds to the weight of the myth of confidence: that confidence is only for the moments when things go in your favour. Again, this is partly to do with our attention span and what we are drawn to. For newspapers and the drivers of internet algorithms, it's not a story to feature a picture of someone who is magnanimous in defeat and feeling open-hearted about their opponent's win, saying, 'Aw, shucks, dem's the breaks. Maybe next time, guys!' This is probably why you might be able to picture the England 'winners' but you can't remember the German 'losers'. However, if they had been photographed looking utterly vengeful, hate-filled and murderous, that would have been a hotly in-demand picture. What makes a story, traditionally speaking? The face of glorious triumph, or the face of the vanquished, broken in defeat, embittered by their opponent's triumph and already displaying the early signs of a sneer of future revenge? The German team were invisible in the mainstream coverage after their defeat largely because they didn't gratify the narrative by being sore losers. Athletic happy high status behaviour takes the drama out of a situation because it reflects acceptance of the outcome – even when the outcome is not in your favour.

'But I thought everyone loves a winner . . .?'

It is a truism that is drummed into us from birth: there can only be one winner. There's nothing more human than celebrating victory, encouraging excellence, promoting competition. It is part of who we are, and without 'wins' there is no arc of progress, whether it's in sport, industry, the arts or business. Of course, we are also told, 'It's not the winning that counts, it's the taking part.' But we all see the reality behind that platitude. It's something we tell the losing side to make them feel better. It's a white lie that reinforces the 'truth'. Losing is bad. Winning is good. After all, you get the most attention and praise when you win, don't you?

Or do you? What if our focus on that polarity is changing, and we're starting to see a bigger picture? What if the 'taking part' platitude is actually being proven to be a more powerful motivator? One of the major narratives emerging from sporting competitions over the past few years is the changing emotional response to the concept of success, driven by a younger generation. For example, the British diver and Olympic gold medallist Tom Daley, born in 1994, is now just as famous for sitting off to the side of the pool twiddling away with his knitting needles as he is for his impressive diving. He credits knitting as his 'super-power' and says it reduces the stress and perfectionism that are prevalent in sport: 'What knitting has taught me is that mistakes can teach you so many lessons . . . I owe my Olympic gold to knitting.' Similarly, at the 2020 Olympics, the gymnast Simone Biles, born in 1997, pulled out of her events to concentrate on her physical and mental health. Of her decision, Alex Bowen, a member of Team USA's men's water polo team, said: 'To be able to overcome your own ego and step aside, that's huge.' Similarly, the average age of the German women's football team is twenty-four. Most of them were born in the late 1990s. There's no way of proving it, but it seems to me that the attitude of these young athletes is different from those who came before them. Yes, they're in it to win it. But not at any cost. This is the definition of athletic happy high status.

Many are still sceptical about the wisdom of this more relaxed attitude to competition and to status. At the Olympics, these kinds of stories sparked heated debate. Some argued that these athletes are 'soft', pampered and spoilt. Others contended passionately that they are actually the opposite of 'soft'. Instead they are almost superhuman in their ability to acknowledge their weakness and normality in the face of intense pressure to live up to an ideal, when they know they are likely to be criticized and scrutinized for doing so. Typical headlines about Simone Biles from the time veered between two extremes, from 'Biles puts her team ahead of her ego' and 'Biles finds winning mix with big skills, small ego' to 'Simone Biles is no hero. She's a quitter' and 'Selfish Biles lets her team down.'

There is a cultural shift happening here. But there is no consensus as to whether it's a good or a bad thing in the long term. However, although I'm not a sports gambler myself, I know which kind of strength I would put my money on: the one that is closer to athletic happy high status. Which means backing athletes who put their team and their mental health ahead of the win. And yet the cultural pull of victory – and 'winning confidence' being the only kind of confidence that counts – is strong. The overcoming of ego and the embracing of something bigger than ego – your own humanity, your own calm, your own well-being – is something we have not seen celebrated or even really acknowledged in public life until the twenty-first century. Which is why there is something fascinating going on when these young high-performers talk about their enlightened attitudes. It's almost like some of them are trying to convince themselves that all that matters is the participation and the experience: to do it for the love of it. But you can't help but think their true desired outcome is still 'to be the best', which is, of course, enhanced by the joy of participation. Therefore the joy of participation is not truly purely for itself, it is in service of a goal. The goal is still excellence – but the excellence is enhanced by being more relaxed and more holistic. This is the double whammy of happy high status: when you are accepting of any outcome and used to being magnanimous in defeat, you usually play better anyway.

This echoes the insights Tom Daley has given into his preparation for the Olympics. He has listed different motivations at different times and they are never anything like 'going for gold' or 'beating everyone else'. Instead they are things like: giving it your best shot, being in the best possible shape, putting yourself under intense pressure, knowing that others support and love you no matter what the outcome ... All healthy, controllable motivations. He lists that last motivation ('no matter what the outcome') as the most satisfying one. He has talked openly at length about the participation increasingly becoming more important to him than the end result.

You even get the sense with Daley's recent interviews that he is genuinely more interested in the purity of enjoyment. Success is a happy, but coincidental, by-product: 'It's not about which medal you win, it's about the attitude you have.' This is another radical way to reframe confidence: by linking it to something that you can control and influence – your enjoyment, your participation, your attitude – instead of linking it to its contribution to 'success'. It's far more satisfying for us to have control over a process, to be able to shape it and relish the challenge of the task in and of itself, than it is for us to throw a dice and cross our fingers for the win. It's corny as hell but it turns out the 'taking part' thing is everything.

There is the same energy in the idea that a happy, balanced, meaningful life is not about small-time, short-term, one-off gains ('I win this argument', 'I land this punch', 'I nail this race'), and that instead it's about your performance, your attitude and your behaviour towards others over the long term. It's a redefinition of the winning mindset that Tom Daley's late father understood long before anyone else: 'If you go into a competition with eighteen people in it and you come last, as long as you do your best, you're eighteenth-best in the whole country. How cool is that?' Athletic happy high status means accepting and celebrating the spot where you've landed and being Zen about it. It is about recognizing that maybe today it's not your turn but that's not the end of the world. It's about judging yourself over the long haul and recognizing that no moment – win or lose – represents the final say on your ability to perform.

There is grace in defeat

Within twenty-four hours of the England–Germany match, I posted two Instagram pictures, one about the optics of England's win ('This is what female success looks like') and the second about Germany's defeat ('This is what female failure looks like'), which provided an insight into our readiness to challenge the obsession with winning.

I hesitated with the second post, which showed that picture of Alexandra Popp, her head bowed. I thought I would get some pushback for featuring women in defeat, for highlighting Germany's experience at a time when England should be in the spotlight, for focusing on names and faces that aren't known, for missing the point. Instead there was the opposite response.

The post about grace in the face of defeat was far more popular and widely shared than the post about the obvious thing: winning. Typical comments: 'Loss and failure are as important an experience as success. And they did it with style.' 'Being number one has got a few women into a few boardrooms, but we need to normalize being number two, three or four and still being considered successful.' 'Women at all parts of the pyramid. Not just the apex.' 'My 11-year-old daughter plays football and, yes, it's brilliant she saw women win. But she needs to learn how losing can be good.' 'Gracious sporting defeat has to be applauded.' 'The credit goes to the man or woman who is actually in the arena.'

This response signals that we're ready for a grown-up societal conversation that goes beyond the empty sloganeering of 'You go, girl' (or whatever patronizing equivalent) and instead focuses on championing the kinds of people we haven't seen *lose* before. It will be interesting to see exactly what this change will entail. Because it will mean losers as well as winners, it will mean perhaps seeing unfamiliar faces being mean, competitive, difficult, aggressive. Not everyone will be as big-hearted as Alexandra Popp. Not everyone will be as relaxed as Tom Daley. Not everyone will be as compassionate as Simone Biles. It will mean us seeing women, in particular, bottle it, lose their temper, struggle, fail. But sometimes it will mean witnessing them when they are able to maintain happy high status even when all the odds are stacked against them – and even when they are publicly at a low point – and recognizing that this is still a form of confidence in both men and women.

Real self-belief looks like stoic defeat or noble failure. It is all very well to feel that boost when we are literally 'happy' in ourselves and everything goes to plan. The true test of the matter is when things go badly. This is when we see how well someone has integrated 'happy' (balanced, calm, at ease) with 'high status' (as ready to lead as to follow, open to possibilities, quietly impressive). This is as relevant at moments of extreme public loss and perceived humiliation – international sporting disaster, political defeat at the national or global level, falling over on stage on your world tour – as it is in those everyday, private moments of disappointment like losing a contract, getting turned down for a job or having to stomach someone you can't stand being asked to do something you really wanted to do. Be sad, sure, because you're human, and by all means be annoyed that it's not your day. But also be proud in the knowledge that you're handling that situation while maintaining your hard-won deep-rooted confidence.

How to get a piece of it

- Find the 'your world' equivalent to these examples. It makes sense to be specific about what your own definition of 'losing' is and how you can handle it with more openness. Very few of us win or lose as publicly or significantly as athletes. But we all have industry definitions of celebration and disaster. The business thinker Margaret Heffernan advises keeping a weekly list of 'invisible wins and losses', a tally sheet where you list between three and five things that have gone well or badly that week, the outcome, and the lesson learned. This is also what tech entrepreneur Abadesi Osunsade calls 'work receipts' – a documentary record of events, comments, data, facts. Are you on top of your 'work receipts'? If you can get into the habit of doing this, you instantly have a note to hand of 'failures survived' (to inspire and motivate yourself) and a crib sheet for a time when you need to prove your track record (to demonstrate your achievements to others).

- Have a support system, whether paid or unpaid, formal or informal. This could be a mentor, a supportive friend or a career coach. But know who it is and make a habit of checking in with them. Perversely, it almost feels as if it's easier to rewrite failure when it's as high-stakes as missing out on an Olympic medal than when it's a small, everyday thing. Of course, Alexandra Popp, Simone Biles and Tom Daley have to master this mentality – it's part of what they do. But the reality is that in a 'normal' job (rather than being, say, a professional footballer or an Olympian athlete) you do not usually have the equivalent of a coach or sports psychologist to help you to identify patterns. In everyday life our goals are much more subjective: we are not working towards a gold medal, we are working towards impressing someone at a marketing meeting or keeping our cool during a professional confrontation. If you struggle long-term with low moments or you can see there are certain patterns recurring in your life, it's worth thinking about having a person or a group of people who tick the 'support' box. In the case of these sporting high achievers – as well as at the top of corporate and performance-driven organizations – this kind of help is part of the fabric of their enterprise. If that's not part of your set-up, sometimes it's enough to note down issues yourself or talk them through with someone who is not annoying. Other times you need a formalized system – like a coach or a mentor appointed to you – in order to make sure change happens.

- Take that Kipling quote about the twin imposters of success and failure as your inspiration and keep a list of moments in your life when successes turned out to have a downside and failures emerged as turning points. This is a way of keeping perspective and staying sane. In sport, you get one chance during one moment and the result is obvious. In most other things in life, it can take weeks, months or years to see if something really was a good idea in the long term. And even in sport, a significant failure can be the building block for a future success.

Inspiration for athletic happy high status: suppressing ego in service of excellence

Traits: Hard-working. Dynamic. Determined in building both physical and mental strength. Puts as much time into 'How to cope with losing' as into 'How to win'. Values effort and competition over outcome and results. Individual performer who can also handle being a team player.

Most useful for: Recovering perfectionists. Anyone who wants to 'win' but is daunted by the downsides of winning or the prospect of the 'near miss'. Players who tend to 'hide' in the team but want to step up.

Who succeeds at this: **Marcus Rashford** – high-performing footballer and role model who puts integrity and long-term social change at the heart of his impact. **Emma Raducanu** – tennis player who publicly models how to treat success and defeat with equal grace. **Sarina Wiegman** – football manager known for being cool, calm and straight-talking. **Adam Peaty** – Olympic swimmer who has spoken openly about managing injuries and staying focused. **Nicola Adams** –

former professional boxer who combines physical strength with softly-spoken gentle energy.

Chapter 9

DON'T BE LIKE ANYONE: BE LIKE YOU

THE PROS AND CONS OF 'JUST BE YOURSELF'

Your Happy High Status:
Unique, One-off, Inimitable

'"Myself" wants to run away.'

How do you make all these variations on happy high status come together and forge your own authentic style? One of the most common pieces of advice any of us will ever receive in relation to our confidence is the infuriating instruction 'Just be yourself.' This three-word neck brace has irritating cousins: 'Just be confident.' 'Just relax.' 'Just go for it.' 'Just do whatever feels right to you.' The most annoying thing about this form of advice is that it is not in and of itself bad advice. In fact it's excellent advice. But only theoretically. It's advice to people who don't need any advice. If you are already being yourself, relaxing and going for it, you should indeed continue with gusto. It's true that if we could 'just be' all these things all the time, the world would be a much better place. The problem is, it is advice that begs a much bigger question: 'How do I "just be" those things if I'm not already doing them naturally? Where do I start?' I might also argue that it is the advice of a person who does not really have any advice to give you. Because helpful advice is way more specific than this foolish generic platitude.

If you're not already a self-assured person, the well-meaning injunction to 'just be yourself' is one of the biggest stumbling blocks to confidence and to your own unique happy high status. Because our responses to it are paralysing. And it feels humiliating. It implies that this is an easy job, that it should come naturally, that there is something wrong with you if you can't 'just relax'. What *is* useful advice is to dig down into the questions prompted by 'Just be yourself': 'What is meant by this?' 'How do we act on this?' 'What does it look like?' 'How do you know you're doing it?' 'What is your "self"?' If you are the person on the receiving end of this advice, it's incredibly tempting to take it literally: 'Just be myself, you say? Well, "myself" is shit scared. Myself wants to get on a plane to Barbados. Myself says, "Help! Someone get me out of this!"' 'You want the real me? The real me is going to go and dig a pit to bury my "self" in. See you outside.'

There is a gap between the authenticity implied by the instruction to 'just be yourself' and the necessity of the inauthentic camouflage usually required to face a pressured situation. Often in moments when we are most required to 'be ourselves' we are least able to, because it would not be socially acceptable to be panicked, tearful, scatty, discombobulated, exhausted, anxious . . . So instead we camouflage: we hide those genuine feelings of fear and dread. When you are in camouflage mode, you cannot 'just be yourself'. It's also a deeply stupid thing to say. I mean, if you could just be yourself, if you could just relax, if you could just be funny, you wouldn't need any advice, would you? That's without mentioning how irritating the word 'just' is here. We wish it were simple and immediate. It isn't. You cannot 'just' be something by wishing it into being.

'Just be yourself' is about the task of authenticity. You'd think that our ability to judge authentic confidence would be second nature, part of being human. But like so many things in life, being 'authentic' or being 'real' and not 'fake' means different things to different people. A seminar report in the *Journal of Education and Learning* in 2020 defined authenticity in the context of educational assessments as being 'real-to-life' or having 'real-life' value. That in itself is problematic: often we are asked to perform confidently at work in situations that have very little real-life value. (Especially meetings.) Even worse, in 2017 Columbia University delivered research into how artificial intelligence may affect our perception of authenticity. They conducted a laboratory project where humans and AI attempted to replicate the same paintings. It's very hard to tell them apart. We think we know authenticity when we see it – but we're not always right.

This is another instance of a quality being in the eye of the beholder. A company called Quantified Communications measured perceptions of a speaker's characteristics using artificial intelligence. Their 2017 research pinpointed passion, clarity and effective visual delivery (body language, eye contact, gestures) as being the qualities most likely to transmit 'authenticity'. But this all comes across as highly subjective and not really, er, quantifiable. And it all feels a bit chicken-and-egg. If you have passion, you'll be authentic. But you can't fake passion any more than you can fake authenticity. All 'Be yourself' really boils down to is: 'Look as if you mean it.' Or, better: 'Actually mean it.'

We're facing a dilemma here, then. How can you be yourself when yourself is the kind of person who definitely doesn't want to do this thing and doesn't mean it? How can you be yourself when this whole thing feels fake and wrong? How can you just relax when you feel deeply uncomfortable? What if you don't mean it and you're not feeling it? Maybe a more useful question to ask yourself is: 'What has to happen for me to really mean this?'

'Just be yourself' is also dangerous because our real, most raw selves are not always the selves that have our best interests at heart. Sometimes we are 'just' extremely angry, completely petrified, murderously stressed, or consumed by lust, jealousy or resentment ... Or all of the above. Sometimes we self-sabotage. Sometimes we are just too tired to do something. Inside this annoying little phrase, though, there is a nugget of usefulness waiting to escape. 'Just be yourself' encompasses the most important principle of your signature happy high status, provided you're willing to approach it with the right amount of nuance and put the time into working out what 'being yourself' really means to you, what it looks like and how it feels when you're in that zone. It means asking yourself: 'What conditions do I require so that I can feel like that about myself?' 'What ideas do I need to let go of?' 'What preparation do I need to do?' 'What kind of environments do I need to avoid?' Surprise, surprise: as the expression implies, 'Being yourself' is about individualism. It suggests a unique quality. It looks different on everyone and has no precedent that you need to emulate. It's wide open and ripe for interpretation. 'Just be yourself' gives you licence to be creative and *do it the way only you can do it.* It reminds you that you do not have to copy anyone else to do a good job. It reminds you that you are enough. It reminds you that there are many situations in life where you *are* just being yourself, and you are loved and appreciated for it without making any effort whatsoever and you didn't even have to think about how to do that. It's reminiscent of the Dolly Parton adage: 'Find out who you are and do it on purpose.' Pinpoint the conditions. Replicate them. Find out who you are when you are your most relaxed, when you are yourself, when you have no self-consciousness . . . And do it on purpose in the moments when it doesn't come naturally.

Personalizing this task of confidence

I can't stress enough how individual each of us is when it comes to these issues. As I suggested earlier, many people are labouring under the (comforting? limiting?) impression that confidence – and, certainly, confidence when you're in front of others – is a standard to which you can conform, a bit like passing an exam. If you revise the right things, learn the right rules, stand like this, say this, write in a notebook with this number of lines and use this many bullet points, then you will get it right. Some people think they've maybe got one thing missing and want to treat it like a jigsaw: just fill in this bit . . . with this piece . . . and *voilà*! Of course, this makes sense up to a point. There are hallmarks of confidence that are common to all of us and that can be studied and learned. But because this is more of an art than a science, those rules can be broken and it can still work. Even better, because it is an art, you can make a lot of it up and do it your way. That is the real route to 'Just be yourself': do it like only you can do it.

As the writer Gretchen Rubin points out in her work about happiness and habits, one principle we struggle to remember in life relates to our similarity to other human beings. In terms of what habits and attitudes benefit and harm us, we are more like other people than we care to admit. But the tiny ways in which we are different in terms of personality and inclination are hugely significant. As Rubin reminds us, there are many aspects to habitual human behaviour where we don't differ hugely: we all need roughly the same amount of sleep, we all like to complete tasks that feel meaningful to us and be around people who make us feel appreciated and acknowledged, we all benefit from brushing our teeth at the same time every day. But we wildly differ in our tastes, our interests and our values. And if we don't pay attention to observing both sides of that equation, we will make ourselves miserable.

When it comes to the first half of the equation, there are basic truths about confidence that relate to all of us. We stand our best chance of being confident when we feel that we are being authentic and acting with integrity. It's harder for us to be confident when we are, say, tired or hungry. Confidence is easier for us in situations that we judge as familiar and unthreatening. Beyond that, the individual variations are as many as there are people on the planet. Gretchen Rubin puts it simply: 'What's fun for other people may not be fun for you.' It sounds obvious but we rarely remember it. It's also true of confidence: what feels like happy high status to you may not be happy high status to others. That counts both for the execution – how you get there – and for the result – what it looks like. The more we consider how self-assurance works for most people, the more we can judge whether that fits with our personal story. Are we an average example who can follow general advice? Or are we an outlier? How much of our behaviour is generalized human behaviour that is common to most people? Where do we differ? This is where 'just being you' starts to emerge.

Preparation is an uncomfortable thing to think about here. The question is often asked in relation to a job inter-view, speech or presentation: 'How much preparation will I need to do in order to feel confident?' I always feel like answering '17.48 hours'. Because it's a ridiculous ques-tion. It depends entirely on what kind of person you are as an individual. Do you enjoy preparation and find it useful? Or does it just make you more nervous? Have you really understood the task in hand or could it be that you're over-preparing and/or preparing for a completely different task? Have you done something like this before? Have you talked to anyone who's done something similar, to see if their means of preparing feels right to you? The right amount of preparation is enough to make you feel reasonably confident but not so much as to make you rigid in what you've prepared.

If you do so much prep that you're wedded to it, you leave little room to 'just be yourself'. You'll be too busy showing the prep. Because often preparation means memorizing, planning, doing the homework, putting the hours in . . . And if others can see and feel that in you, already your authenticity is lost. Know what kind of preparation suits you. And camouflage your preparation – no one wants to know that you've done nothing and you're winging it, and no one wants to feel the weight of the hundreds of hours of preparation you put in. Some people's confidence is ruined by over-preparation. Others' is destroyed by under-preparation. Know yourself. Personalize. Don't take for granted things that may be true for others but aren't necessarily true for you.

The trick is to study your own habits and strengths, and be honest with yourself about what is realistic and attractive for you individually, without getting bogged down in the generic. Do not universalize the task. That will make it feel difficult. Make it about you. That will make it feel easy. For example, yes, it's a generic truth that many people find presenting and public speaking stressful. No one's denying that. But setting that truth to one side, if you were to do it your way and feel like yourself while doing it, what would that look like? What might you need to get there? How could it be done? To return to the example of

Greta Thunberg, she clearly sets herself manageable parameters. She might have a cue card with bullet points. She might memorize one statistic. She will leave long pauses after she has made a point. These things aren't accidental: they are brilliant examples of her personalizing the task. But they aren't rules, either. Someone else in the same situation might feel more confident handling each moment as it arises, without sticking to a script. They might 'just be themselves' by keeping it fresh and unpredictable.

It's so important to recognize that confidence doesn't mean schooling yourself in formalities and conforming to a standard as if other people have been to some weird imaginary confidence school and you haven't. Finding your own signature happy high status means bending the situation to your needs and your strengths. If you hate the idea of standing up in front of people, get a chair or a high stool to sit on. If you hate looking people in the eye, don't wear your glasses. Or if you don't wear glasses, make fake eye contact (look at their noses or elbows) or find a point in the room and fill it with a hologram of someone you love. If you hate memorizing text, read out part of what you're going to say and speak the rest as if you were speaking to a friend.

Challenge your own preconceptions about what is expected. Do you know for sure that there's only one accepted way of doing things? If you want to do something unusual or out of the ordinary and it feels wrong or scary, ask yourself how you would feel if someone else did that thing. Would it really be so weird? Or might it be refresh-ing and different? A friend of mine recently had to speak at a funeral and was getting worried about expressing too much emotion and bursting into tears. But when he began to consider what he would expect from someone else in that position, he had to acknowledge that emotion and tears were not only not to be avoided, they were surely to be encouraged. Where else are you going to show emotion and tears? As soon as he flipped that idea and saw it from the angle of the congregation rather than the point of view of the speaker, it transformed how he approached the task and he was able to 'be himself'. Personalize your response to the situation and mould it so that it sits comfortably with you. You are not missing a trick. No one else knows how to 'be you' better than you do.

Project yourself into a bright future (even if it makes you cringe)

You know – better than anybody else – what a future ver-sion of yourself might be able to accomplish. The ability to visualize your own authenticity in the future and picture a successful outcome is priceless. This sounds like some kind of creepy self-hypnosis, but wishful thinking is a tried and tested formula for success. One of the most promising research paths to emerge in recent years – and one that is hugely helpful to developing a concept of happy high status – is the idea that people who *think more about them-selves in the future than they do about themselves in the past* are more likely to feel confident and optimistic. This is based on an extensive study of PTSD and war veterans by East Tennessee State University in 2019 and is called 'positive future time perspective'. Researchers studied veterans who were able to reframe their experiences, embrace 'future-oriented thinking' and engage in acceptance and commitment therapies. These veterans accepted and processed what had happened to them, instead of simply remembering and reliving it. They were then far more likely to establish healthy sleep patterns and recover from their PTSD.

It might seem extreme to extrapolate ideas around our own confidence from a study like this. I'm no war veteran, unless you count watching multiple episodes of *The A-Team* in the 1980s. But this theory makes sense to me. When I have talked to readers and listeners about their anxieties around public speaking, pay negotiation, job interviews and social interactions of all kinds, they report symptoms and use language that are synonymous with trauma and extreme stress. It would be preposterous to suggest that those feelings and experiences are comparable to those within a war zone. But it's all stress and anxiety, just on a sliding scale. I know from my own early experiences in comedy that when you experience something even mildly traumatic on stage, you amplify it afterwards and replay it in your mind, far more than you do with a positive experience. I learned to 'un-train' myself from having this unhelpful habit by using audio and video evidence of my own performances. If you can listen to or watch yourself objectively, you can see from the outside what 'really' happened, and what was visible or audible to others. You can make a note of what you need to learn, and you can move on. You don't stay stuck living in those feelings, which may in any case not be a reflection of objective reality. Often I would come off-stage full of anxiety and annoyance because I had 'missed a bit' and forgotten to do a piece of material that I meant to perform. But that wasn't visible to anyone else and I was just spoiling it for myself. I learned to do those 'bits that I might forget' early on or not bother about them at all. It often turned out that maybe they wanted to be forgotten for a reason.

It's important to remember that this 'trauma' of audience scrutiny, the weight of the attention of others, affects everyone's nervous system. Getting over it and treating it with equanimity requires exposure, experience and time. Even on the *How to Own the Room* podcast, where I interview individuals who are usually extremely outwardly successful – often world-famous, wealthy and high-achieving – there's a significant percentage of guests who have used beta blockers to reduce blood pressure or sought hypnotherapy or other clinical help to overcome anxiety around live performance. And these are often people who are actually doing public speaking for a living – sometimes on tour in front of tens of thousands, or on live television in front of millions – and who appear 'effortlessly confident'. Again: there's no secret that everyone is in on apart from you.

Being yourself when things go wrong

A major challenge to authenticity is when we are angered, threatened, humiliated, or even simply when our patience is tested in front of others. This can happen very easily in situations where we are under pressure to be confident. We've all seen it on stage. The slides don't work. The clicker doesn't work. Someone mispronounces a name or announces someone as the wrong person. Or there's a mishap in the room: a door slams, a fire alarm goes off, there's a light that won't stop flickering. I've been on stage when someone in the audience has had a stroke and the event has had to be stopped to let in an ambulance crew. Your job in these situations is to, yes, 'just be yourself'. But you had better be your most proportionate, reasonable and serenely swan-like self. The mere possibility of these situations occurring is enough to make some people say no to even very low-key and low-pressure opportunities: the fear of the unknown, the uncontrollable, the unpredictable.

But I want you to remember that these are situations where people really will be on your side. In the case of the ambulance drama, this was the first and only time this has happened to me, but I knew enough to ask myself: 'What do people need from me right now as the host?' They needed calm and clarity. So that was all I had to find. In these moments it is really not about you. It is about how everyone else is feeling. They don't want to feel sorry for you. They don't want to see you lose your temper because the event has gone pear-shaped. They want to see that you are a nice person who knows that things go wrong sometimes and it's not a big deal. Is that really so frightening?

As we've already explored through the principles of narrative, and through characters on stage and on screen, sometimes you can find the happy high status response by asking: 'How good a story is this going to make?' If the answer is: 'A very boring one that no one would want to hear' then that is very likely a productive path of action in real life for when things go wrong. Don't throw the clicker when your slides freeze. Don't say, 'Oh my God, someone has had a stroke.' Don't mutter, 'I can't believe this is happening to me.' These reactions might be authentic. But they are not confident.

The happy high status reaction is the reaction of a person who is not seeking to cause headlines or drama, who is not choosing a behaviour that makes us shocked or impressed or awed or intimidated. The behaviour might occur in the spotlight and in the presence of others but it does not self-consciously seek the spotlight or the approval of others. This is a major source of confusion about confidence: that the only way to display it is to seek the spotlight – and that is an off-putting and frightening thing for many people. Plus, we can also have a distaste for people who actively seek the spotlight, so it feels doubly uncomfortable. But the spotlight itself is neutral. And you can behave with balance, neutrality, authenticity, kindness and openness in it. Being put on the spot does not transform you into an attention-seeking monster. And attention-seeking monsters need not be the only people who thrive and feel comfortable when they're on the spot.

Happy high status is more valuable than authenticity

Off-stage, without hundreds of eyes glaring at us, it can still serve us better to park our authentic response to high-pressure situations and dig deep to find a happy high status one. After all, even if we're not on show in a professional sense, we know in our own minds from moment to moment whether we have behaved in a way that is happy high status or not. Often in our personal lives and in our everyday interactions, it can feel harmless or even vindicating to behave however we feel like behaving, to go with our feelings. Because isn't that being authentic? Well, yes and no. Happy high status is about seeking solutions that are balanced and harmonious, and in our long-term best interests, rather than reacting unthinkingly in the moment.

Obviously we cannot keep our emotions in check all the time. And there is a school of thought that it is somehow justified to react however we want, as long as it's assertive and authentic. But this is an oversimplification. A video was widely shared on social media recently of a mother who had confronted her child's bully. If your child is on the receiving end of bullying – provided it's not a violent incident where you need to call the police – you might be looking to channel some variation of happy high status in order to find a resolution. This woman did not do this.

Instead she summoned the bully's mother and the bullying child to a meeting. When the bully's mother denied the behaviour, the mother who called the meeting hit her in the face. ('And so I popped her.') As her target reeled in shock and fear, the mother bent down and said to the bullying child: 'See? Your mother cannot defend herself from me. So think about that before you bully my child again.' She walked away, leaving both bully and bully's mother in tears. She alleges in the video that this was a 'brilliant solution' as no further bullying occurred. Hmm.

This behaviour could be seen as 'confident' and 'authentic', but is this happy high status? Clearly not. Popping someone – however deserved – is never happy high status. The appropriate 'confident' response to this situation is not an easy one to discern. But it's definitely not this reaction. This video makes for one great story, though, and one almighty talking point. A video of a parent expressing the following (boring but sensible) sentiment would not be widely shared: 'My child was bullied and I asked the teacher to intervene and sort it out on their terms, and I had the patience to wait it out and it was a great learning experience for everyone.' In reality, all the viral video teaches is that the only way to deal with a bully is to out-bully them.

Often we're privately drawn to solutions that will give us a rush of adrenaline, a feeling of righteousness, a sense of revenge. Sometimes we mistake that for 'confidence'. If you're still thinking that the woman in the video did 'the right thing' then consider the factors we don't know. We don't know that her child had not provoked the situation. We don't know the family set-up of the child who was a bully. They might be experiencing violence at home. We don't know that every single adult involved here is not violent in other situations. We don't really know anything. It's tedious and tricky and goody-goody to hold all these possibilities in our minds when we weigh up a 'confident' response to a stressful situation. But in choosing to lower the stakes, to reserve judgement, to give ourselves time to weigh things up from a different angle, we have the chance of fixing things rather than simply reacting emotionally to a given problem.

Giving in to revenge is what Michelle Obama, in an echo to the line in her famous speech, calls 'an attitude of low'. It is very tempting to allow your state of mind, your belief in yourself, your motivation or your happy high status to be swayed by comments, events and circumstances outside of yourself. It's entirely human to have that impulse, especially when it feels like you are 'just being yourself'. But ultimately it's empty: by responding to a stressor in this way, you are allowing someone else to define who you are. By this measure, you will also always be waiting for someone else to validate you, or to give you a reason to speak out or, conversely, to convince you that, yes, you should have stayed silent, and you don't deserve to speak. It's not so much about 'rising above it' as avoiding the temptation of going low. If you can't stay high, at least don't go low. Stay in neutral and wait for more information. As Michelle Obama concluded in an interview:

'It's not about denying the rage. It's not about being complacent . . . When I think about going high, I think about, *What is my point? What is my ultimate goal?* . . . We can't live in low. It doesn't help our souls.' This isn't for everyone. The interviewer, TV presenter Gayle King, laughed at Michelle's comment and referenced an exchange in the reality TV show *The Real Housewives of Atlanta* where one woman said to another, 'I'm not Michelle Obama. When you go low, I'm going low with you.' We can't all be happy high status. But we can at least know if we're trying.

How to get a piece of it

- Try to reframe the instruction to 'just be yourself'. Find a way of fulfilling the task in hand that feels very comfortable to you. Ahead of time, think about how things could be tweaked so that you feel more at home and more supported. How much preparation do you need to 'be yourself'? How much freedom or flexibility do you need? Very often, people are pointlessly and falsely constrained by norms, standards and habits that have no good reason behind them and that no one actually wants you to adopt. Don't let the expectation of norms unsettle you. There is no norm other than the one you impose. For instance, any time I do a show or a presentation, I will receive this question: 'What are your tech requirements? Let us know URGENTLY.' The fact is, I don't really have any, except maybe a microphone (and in some cases a mic stand, but even that I can live without). But the question used to always make me think: 'Oh no. I don't have any tech requirements. Perhaps I had better come up with some and FAST.' But the truth is: I don't have any and I don't need to have any. The person is only asking the question because it is their job to do so, not because they care if you have any tech requirements or not: they're not trying to signal that tech requirements are a necessity. It's like that question you get asked before a meal in any restaurant, 'Do you have any allergies?' You are not required to have allergies.

- Accept that there are situations where it is very difficult – actually, impossible – to 'be yourself'. Situations where being 'authentic' is a bad move professionally or where it's just not achievable. Examples of this include: if you are delivering information that absolutely anyone could deliver; if you are filling in for someone else; if you are in a professional situation you can't excuse yourself from on a day when you are feeling very emotional or sick; if you are trapped in a job you hate in order to earn money. Sometimes you just have to do the best job you can and let it be whatever it is. In these kinds of situations there are two fixes. One, short-term: grin and bear it, and try to do the least fake job you can. Two, long-term: work towards escaping these situations. There is a place for 'be yourself' but not in every part of our lives. Allow yourself to be a harmless 'white lie' version of yourself from time to time. (Obviously I'm not telling you to become a duplicitous fake in order to stomach your own life. That is a bad idea.)

- There is one supremely useful tip to extrapolate from 'Just be yourself.' If you are ever facing a situation where it would be appropriate to say or do something that *no one else on the planet* could contribute: then do or say that thing. Naturally it needs to be appropriate to the context. So if you're supposed to be talking about emerging markets in China, you can't start really talking about your experience as a goatherd on your gap year. (Or maybe you can. I mean, I

don't want to stifle anyone's creativity here.)
But if you can bring a unique perspective or
personal experience or an original argument,
*especially if no one else could say this thing
because they are not you*, this can be an
incredibly helpful thing to introduce. Think:
'What can I tell them that no one else can tell
them?' This also works for energy: 'What
energy can I bring that no one else can
bring?' And experience: 'How is my
experience different from anyone else's? How
can I apply that?' You can really have
confidence in these situations because no one
can contradict, copy or challenge your
energy or experience if it is unique to you. It
is also grounding and reassuring when you
are experiencing self-doubt. What are they
lucky to have from you that no one else could
bring? If you were missing, what else would
be missing?

• Keep going back over the first exercise in this
book: experience your feelings and self-image
when you are 'inside' that memory of a
moment of pride, triumph, competence, joy.
You can take that experience and those
feelings, and 'overlay' them in any situation.

(Any situation within reason. In some situations we have to break and cry and scream and grieve. Be realistic.) When you feel yourself being overwhelmed, or hijacked by nerves or anxiety, dip into that feeling. See if there is anything inside that memory of yourself that you can import into this situation. It is very easy to descend into black-and-white thinking, especially when we are facing something that challenges our confidence. We can start to think: 'I'm not up to this.' 'I can't do this.' 'I can't cope.' But those memories and instances of excellence and joy are real in our lives. We have all had moments where we could do it and we could cope easily. Yes, this challenging situation will be different from those moments. But you are the same person. Bring that 'coping' version of yourself to the party.

Inspiration for your happy high status: unique, one-off, inimitable

Traits: It doesn't feel effortful. It feels uncomplicated. It feels like you can be the same person no matter who you're talking to. You don't question yourself or overanalyse. You're not too 'in your head'.

Most useful for: Anyone. Especially anyone who is sick of faking it or of feeling envious of the confidence of others.

Who succeeds at this:

You already do – effortlessly . . .

When you are **with people you trust.**

When you are **well rested and well prepared.**

When you are **relaxed in mind and body.**

When you are **unthreatened and have no reason to fear.**

When you know **you can contribute something useful to others.**

How can you transfer these circumstances – and the emotions they evoke – to more situations?

Chapter 10

HAPPY HIGH STATUS FOR LIFE

REMINDING YOURSELF OF THE STAKES AND ALLOWING YOURSELF TO BE ENTITLED

Challenging the status quo

What if you still feel afraid to put these ideas into action? And what if you feel the weight of all the factors that are stacked up against you? Well, you wouldn't be alone in those feelings. We are schooled in avoiding confrontation, giving in to authority and knowing our place. In 2022 the *Journal of Experimental Psychology: Applied* published the results of research into 'social power'. This study was called 'Sorry, Not Sorry' and aimed to examine the role of our preconceptions about power and apology. The test subjects were faced with a 'high-power transgressor'. Most of them quickly reasoned that they were talking to someone who was likely to wriggle out of responsibility, to pass the buck and say the equivalent of 'sorry, not sorry', so there wasn't much point in taking them to task in the first place. The study concluded – guess what? – that in most interactions, if we perceive that the 'high-power transgressor' (the person we want to speak out against) is likely to engage in excuses and shift the blame, we will be less likely to speak out against them. In other words: once you are high status, your status or seniority shields you from criticism and challenges. It ended up proving that our pre-conceptions are pretty damn accurate: before we challenge someone of 'high power', we make a calculation in our minds about whether they will listen, take responsibility and say sorry. If we think they won't, we dodge the challenge, we don't waste our breath. This is how power maintains power: our instinct is to avoid conflict when we think the status quo will prevail anyway.

This is a depressing finding, but in the face of this fact, the need to use 'happy high status' (individual, chosen power – which anyone can have) to challenge high status (institutionalized, conferred power – which only a few can have) couldn't be more important. So how does this uncomfortable information help us shift our feelings of reluctance when it comes to asserting ourselves? Well, once we know and acknowledge something is a proven phenomenon, we can do something to break out of the 'predictable' human behaviour. We get to analyse whether we want to do the predictable thing or we want instead to think for ourselves. We have choice and agency, and we can make decisions about our instinctive behaviour instead of being ruled by it. Once you are aware of this example, you can think to yourself: 'I'm not falling for that old chestnut. This person deserves to be challenged and I'm not going to let them wriggle out of it.' That is how the narrative is changed. That is how we raise our status.

Unfortunately, though, these analyses of power, relationships and fear rarely seem to motivate us to change. The findings of studies of human behaviour – like the

'Sorry, Not Sorry' experiment – can be used in two ways. Either to break free from – or question the wisdom of – the 'expected' behaviours that they document, or to give yourself an excuse: 'Oh well, I behave this way because everyone does . . . I guess there's no point in changing.' The first way is happy high status and is hard work. The second allows you to stay safe in your little box. Studies that back up our fears and our power dynamics gain cultural traction fast: we like telling ourselves that we 'can't help' how we feel and that 'this is how most people feel so it must be OK'. For example, in any conversation about fear and anxiety, someone will usually mention the idea that our fear of speaking in public ranks higher than our fear of death. It's supposed to be our number-one fear. Not that we are afraid we will die, but that we will be alive . . . and our confidence will fail us. This comes from the 1973 'American Fears' study (but I think we can safely assume that these fears are a good indication of universal fears, they're not exclusive to Americans). This study, perhaps more than any other, has led to the overriding belief that it's normal – or even expected – to lack confidence, especially around other people.

At the time, the study's findings led to the famous headline: 'Public Speaking is Worse Than Death for Most of Us'. Let's allow that to sink in: *worse than death for most of us*. It's a powerful idea. Just thinking about something being worse than death is enough to put you off it. I mean, why risk something *worse than death for most of us*? No wonder the confidence myth is so persistent. It's fifty years since that study, and in theory we should be a lot more confident now than we were then. We live in a world where any of us can start our own channel on YouTube. We talk to each other routinely on video screens. But this seems to have made a lot of people *more* self-conscious, not less. The myth persists. The prospect of losing face – putting ourselves in a situation where everyone is looking at us and we have to find the confidence to 'deliver' – is commonly understood to be terrifying.

But if that study result sounds overblown and hyperbolic, that's because – guess what? – it is. The headline – which has become received wisdom and is frequently repeated as a fact, even five decades on – exaggerated the results of the research and misrepresented them. In fact, public speaking only ranked '*amongst* the top six fears'. Not *worse than death*. When survey participants were asked to rank their utmost top fear, they consistently and very sensibly said: 'Death'. And it was actually the fear of the loss of a family member – not the fear of public speaking – that came a close second. This is also sensible and consistent with any kind of sane answer. But 'amongst our top six fears' is not such a great headline, is it?

When you properly think about this widely accepted claim, it makes sense that it was never true. Most people do not think this. Most people are rightly far more terrified of death or of the loss of a loved one. Of course human beings are not self-centred sociopaths who would rather experience the death of a relative than talk in front of other people. It's quite amusing to me that people believed this so easily. And yet it reveals a truth: believing that speaking in front of others is the worst, most scary thing in the world gives us a good enough excuse *not* to do it. We know that we cannot avoid death. But we can say, 'No, thanks, I'd rather not do that presentation. Ask Brian. He is more confident at these things.' We want evidence that shows it's legitimate and correct to fear loss of face. We want stories, information, data, myths that back up the instinct to hide. When we get this 'evidence' – even when it's inaccurate and misrepresented – we share it and repeat it and lap it up because it confirms something that we think we know: that to do anything exposing or vulnerable or exciting or risky is more terrifying than death. We want to believe it because it validates our excuses. 'Can't you ask someone else?' 'I'm not good at that.' 'I'm not confident enough.' 'I'd rather attend my own funeral.'

The truth is, we have far greater fears to worry about than minor challenges to our ego. And if we could all just calm down and settle into that feeling of happy high status then the response would be different: 'I have some under-standable nerves around doing this. But, yes, I can do it.' Our instinct to believe in the intensity of that fear is what the life coach Martha Beck calls 'story-fondling' – it's a comfort blanket and we like to think we need it. So we keep on telling the story ('I'm not confident', 'I'm too scared to do that', 'I am not someone who speaks up') and the more we 'fondle' that blanket of a story, the more comforting it grows until we think we can't possibly do without it. But it's just a story. And it isn't even true.

The moments when we need to be entitled

I am especially, perhaps obsessively, passionate about the role happy high status plays in allowing us to speak up, to move through life without self-doubt and to think, 'Yes, I can.' This is because of something that happened in my own family. Growing up, I was very close to my grandparents – my father's parents. We had many conversations about how they had lived through the number-two worst fear on that list. When they were young parents, in the late 1940s, their first child died in infancy. This was my father's older sister, who died of meningitis just before her third birthday. If you know anyone who has had to bury their child, you will know that is the definition of the worst thing in life. They had no warning and no preparation: their daughter died within two days of falling ill.

It is not so much the fact of this loss, or the effect of it on our family, that has shaped my own thoughts about, and obsession with, confidence and speaking up. It is the circumstances in which this loss occurred. In short: their daughter was misdiagnosed and my grandparents didn't ask for a second opinion, even though they wanted to. They were told she had flu and would be fine. Their gut instinct told them that something was seriously wrong, and it wasn't just the flu. But they didn't know how to challenge the doctor. Within twenty-four hours it was too late.

Their experience illustrates a very simple truth. *Speaking up* is not *worse than death*. It's the other way round. *Not speaking up* is worse than death. If you speak up, the worst thing that can happen is that you lose face a little and you learn something. If you don't speak up, the consequences can live with you for a very long time. Forty years later, when I was a child, my grandparents were still talking about that regret and what could have been. Since then, I've spent a long time considering it. Why are there moments when we argue our corner and moments when we are silent? What makes us lose our confidence in the moments when it matters most? And what if we could make sure that we never bottle it? Just in case. Because there might come a day – as that day was – when the stakes are higher than we know.

There were also a lot of elements related to status, class and hierarchy in my grandparents' story. The doctor who misdiagnosed their child was a stranger, a locum making a house call. It's hard to question someone of status, especially when we don't know them. This man was a military doctor and wearing a uniform. My grandad had served in the RAF during the war a few years previously, and this man outranked him. Plus, a doctor is by definition an educated person. My grandparents were not. They were living above a pub. It's unlikely the doctor lived above a pub. Years later, my grandma remembered this man as being dismissive of their fears and slightly drunk. It was after lunch on a Sunday. It's hard to challenge the hypocrisy of this situation. Supposedly this person knows better than you and you are meant to listen to their educated advice. But in reality they are distracted and are probably a bit tipsy. Not that you can prove that. And they will almost certainly deny it. These are all tiny details of context that don't appear to add up to much. But in the end, paying attention to these kinds of details makes up the difference between respectfully biting your tongue and raising your status to find the presence of mind to say, 'Wait. You are not listening to me.'

The difficulty with prioritizing confidence, assertiveness, happy high status – or whatever we want to call it – in our lives is that this can seem an abstract project, perhaps even self-indulgent or narcissistic. We don't imagine that we will face a moment like the moment that my grandparents faced, where suddenly we need to find a well of courage. This is why confidence is not a luxury or an optional extra. It is a necessity. Anyone can see what the everyday, low-stakes gains of confidence might be – more opportunities, maybe more money, better peace of mind in stressful situations, being able to be a better role model to our colleagues or to our children . . . But we also need to bear in mind what the high-stakes cost is of *not* developing this part of ourselves. Because it can be monumental. And that is a great motivator. So the idea that public speaking is *worse than death for most of us*? That we would rather die than assert ourselves? I don't think so. This is why everyone deserves to be happy high status. So that when the moment comes, it's second nature to stand your ground. And this is why confidence should belong to everyone and not only to certain people. You never know when you might need it – urgently – in a very large dose.

Nobody cares if you mess up, anyway

When I first started performing stand-up comedy ten years ago, I didn't really think much about this story of my grandparents. I was more focused, to my detriment, on my own ego. I stressed about superficial, selfish things like handling heckles, remembering long monologues and coping with negative criticism (and, sometimes, excessively positive feedback, which can be just as toxic and difficult to live with as the bad stuff). These were the worries that kept me up at night. And at the time they really mattered to me, as every time I died on stage, I experienced physical pain. And even though I could feel that pain lessening as time went by, and even though I was learning fast and the humiliations were becoming fewer and further between, still I wanted to minimize the pain and speed up the learning. You do need to learn how to handle all those things. But I was blind to the fact that they get learned through experience and muscle memory, not through overanalysis. If I could go back, I would tell myself to chill out. And I would stop 'story-fondling'. Most things are like learning to ride a bicycle. You are going to have to fall off a few times. Stressing out about falling off is not going to make you learn any faster.

As I progressed and improved, and had more open conversations with other people about how other performers managed all this, I realized that my pursuit of this knowledge really stemmed from that one moment in my grandparents' life. This was the bridge between the 'performance confidence' I was trying to access and the 'real-life confidence' that failed my grandparents on that day. It's all related. As a performer, I was obsessed with the question of authentic confidence and how it could be accessed in moments when I felt low because I was tired, ill or just having a bad day. Because no matter how good you are or how confident you are, you are always going to have days like those. I realized that our everyday reliance on status and self-esteem isn't just for stage. It's for real life, too. I became desperate to figure out what we can do to prevent ourselves from getting stuck in these unnecessary traps of unworthiness, self-doubt and 'not good enough'. Because, after all, what had stopped my grandparents from saying what was on their minds was the exact-same mental block that stops many people from stepping up and doing the things that they want to do, say or be in everyday life.

It's the exact-same mental block that performers, politicians, broadcasters and speakers – people who are hugely experienced and successful – talk about. In acting, you might call it stage fright or 'a dry' – when you forget the next line. In everyday life you might call it self-censorship or biting your tongue. It all comes from the same place: a fear of judgement, of backlash, of impropriety, of negative consequences of some kind. It represents a failure of confidence and of self-trust. It's a fear that grips us even when we don't have any real evidence that the terrible thing we are dreading might come to pass. And worst of all, it is often a self-fulfilling prophecy. Because if you are gripped with the fear that you will be nervous, you are already nervous. Which is why the second most rubbish advice after 'Just be yourself' is 'Don't be nervous.'

What has become increasingly evident to me after years of performing comedy, doing hundreds of gigs for television and radio, and recording endless hours of podcast content is that this fear is entirely misplaced. Even when you underperform, get things badly wrong, misspeak, make major factual errors, say incredibly stupid things or are not remotely funny when you're up on stage as a comedian ... no one actually cares. Or if they do, it's momentary. Perhaps you make an apology and you move on. Or you refund a ticket and it's forgotten. You correct a factual error. You laugh at yourself, you pick yourself up. Even when the thing you fear the most happens and you are revealed to be that thing (stupid, ignorant, incapable, miscast, idiotic, unfunny, uppity, rude . . .), there is usually no major consequence whatsoever.

The world does not end. Nobody dies. That knowledge is incredibly freeing. We all deserve to make the most of it. And without wanting to hit you over the head with the lesson of my grandparents' story, I might as well spell it out: the unimaginable happened and it could not be undone. They accepted the perceived necessity for silence, for acquiescence. And there was a terrible consequence that they had to live with for the rest of their lives. I cannot bear for anyone else to come even close to that situation, especially when I know from personal experience that when you do face the dread and overcome it, your fears are rarely justified. When you speak up, risk something and grab confidence from some deep place within yourself that you didn't even know existed, at worst someone will say, 'Who are you to say that?' And you can think to yourself (or say out loud): 'Well, who am I not to?' It is a profound lesson about entitlement and 'knowing your place'. Or, rather, discovering the happy high status part of you that refuses to know your place.

Put an end to wasting time on insecurity

Perhaps you're still thinking that this detail of my grandparents' life seems poignant and revealing but that it's incidental and specific to them. That they just had a really bad day, the worst kind of day, and that kind of day is not going to happen to everyone. And in a way you'd be right. But is that moment where we feel socially paralysed and our confidence deserts us really that specific and really that rare a phenomenon? I don't think so. I see this story playing out in thousands of tiny ways every day. I see people turning down opportunities, making excuses, waiting to become more confident but never really doing the work to make it happen. I see people everywhere who are, in adulthood, still playing out the narratives of their adolescence, still trapped in the game of 'in' crowd and 'out' crowd, waiting for others to gift them a role in life instead of grabbing the thing they really want without waiting for permission.

This lesson is not historic or unique to my grandparents,

or even to the thinking and to the class issues of their generation. This kind of self-effacement is something that is still happening every day. I hear people all the time saying that they can't answer back in certain situations, that they're giving away their power, minimizing their involvement, paralysed with fear, anxiety or self-loathing. How many times have you swallowed a perfectly good question because 'it might sound stupid'? It's true that none of us can completely influence what happens to us in life and we are not uniquely in charge of our destiny. Limitations are everywhere, structural inequalities are everywhere. Fate can screw any of us over any day of the week. But if that's true, why put more limitations on ourselves? We deserve at least to be free of those.

Many people think they are perhaps relatively happy feeling unconfident and going through life avoiding situations and swallowing their questions for fear of being made to feel stupid. But as we've seen, there can be consequences. Keeping yourself small, respecting authority or leaving a doubt unvoiced is at the very least another time we haven't stood up for ourselves. It's another time we haven't made our presence felt or our opinion known. It's another time we have retreated into that lie: 'I just didn't quite have the confidence.' A life without confidence, without inhabiting your own 'happy high status', is a life half-lived. The lessons in this book help us discover what might happen if we stopped wasting so much energy on silencing ourselves and learned to really, deeply trust ourselves.

When we are in a state of happy high status, we do not need to worry about controlling everything and keeping ourselves 'safe'. Having a robust self-image is not about getting your own way at all costs, bending everything to your will and making sure that everyone else does as you say and that nothing bad ever happens to you. Those things are impossible. But it is about being able to know that if you need to challenge a decision, change your mind or voice a doubt, even if you make a mistake or overstretch, you can weather it easily and without fear of dire consequences. It's about being able to go to sleep at night safe in the knowledge that you've been truly yourself, you've said your piece and you've tried your best. That's the most any of us can ever do.

The example of my grandparents also reflects something important about the inability to speak up and to channel our confidence: it's not always gendered. Of course, this phenomenon is often influenced by factors around gender, class, status, social expectations or structural inequalities. But in this case, it affected both of my grandparents equally: it's not that my grandma was unable to speak up because she was a woman. They were both equally mute, silenced and cowed in that moment. Neither of them had status or agency. They were both 'outranked'. To experience the weight of that failing is human and universal. If we can accept that and recognize it not as a personal failing but as something that anyone would find tough, then we can find a way out of it. There are as many ways to respond to that weight as there are people on the planet. We can respond gracefully, forcefully, with anger, with quiet sadness. We can say: 'I want to say something right now but I can't find the words. Give me a moment.' Or: 'This isn't right. Let me tell you why.' Or even simply: 'We will have to agree to disagree. This is the end of the conversation.' We can always find the words, even if it is going to take us a moment or a breath to do so, and even if it comes out as weaker or angrier than we thought. It's not a small or insignificant thing to find it difficult to speak your mind and stand up for yourself. But we must find the courage to overcome that difficulty. Because if we can't fully express ourselves, we risk living a life that is smaller than the life we were supposed to lead.

There's a saying in psychotherapy: 'Teach people how to treat you.' Unless we are conscious about expressing how we want to be treated, we can find ourselves being treated badly. What that doctor taught my grandparents that day was that he could do his job badly and there would be no consequences for him. They, unwittingly, in return, taught him that they could be treated dismissively. If you teach people that you are a victim or a doormat or a soft touch or a patsy or an easy mark or available for being talked down to or 'not confident', they will treat you that way. If you teach people that you are too scared to challenge authority, even if sometimes that authority is blatantly abused, the person in authority will ride roughshod over you. But if you teach people that you are strong, that you have boundaries, that you won't take no for an answer or that when you say no you mean no, that you don't suffer fools gladly, that you never lend money, that you're sorry but you can't come, that you're too busy to take on that project, that you've had enough and you're willing to state that fact, that you might not be loud and extrovert but you do in fact have a deep inner well of confidence . . . Then they will take you at face value.

When we embrace happy high status, we don't even have to think these things through. We get into the habit of speaking up without asking ourselves whether it's OK to speak up. And it goes without saying that we also feel confident being silent at times, listening extra hard, making space for others, holding back or keeping our counsel, because we trust ourselves to know that's the right thing to do at that time. We feel more free to act and more free to be ourselves. When we are silent, it is out of choice not out of obligation. Who doesn't want a piece of that? The only thing standing in our way is our willingness to have the guts to operate from a place of happy high status instead of a place of fear. Don't waste any more time in hesitating to cultivate it.

Resources, Recommended Reading and Random Thoughts

As I stated in the introduction, this is not an academic book so I didn't want to include a bibliography and lots of footnotes. I do, however, want to make it easy to explore the ideas I have introduced here, so I have used the following notes to trace some of my own thinking and to allow you to follow up on some of the references with further watching, listening and reading. For more updates and ideas, go to my website (https://vivgroskop.com) or sign up to my weekly newsletter (https://howtoowntheroom.com).

Introduction

For anyone else who is as irritated by the idea of 'fake it till you make it' as I am, I recommend two antidotes: *Permission to Speak: How to Change What Power Sounds Like, Starting With You* by Samara Bay (Penguin Business, 2023) and *Find Your Voice: The Secret to Talking with Confidence in Any Situation* by Caroline Goyder (Vermilion, 2020).

It's worth watching footage of Chris Rock's immediate reaction after the famous Oscars slap for a real-life example of keeping your cool in highly pressured and complicated circumstances. (YouTube link: https://www.youtube.com/watch?v=myjEoDypUD8) It's also worth noting how that reaction is second nature to him: every moment of his career in stand-up prepared him for it. In his 2023 Netflix special, *Chris Rock: Selective Outrage*, released a year later, he goes deeper into the reasons why a happy high status reaction was accessible to him. Rock puts his sense of self down to his parents, his upbringing and the expectations that were placed on him. He talks about how he realized in that moment that people were watching him and expecting better.

For a brilliant example of the kind of written content that matches happy high status delivery in a speech, take a look at *A Message from Ukraine* by Volodymyr Zelenskiy (Hutchinson Heinemann, 2022), a collection of Zelenskiy's most powerful speeches. Zelenskiy is always focused on concise, simple, memorable statements delivered with informality and authenticity. People who struggle with happy high status might find it useful to study the language and the rhythm here. This is also a lesson we discussed on the *How to Own the Room* podcast episode with Sarah Hurwitz, Michelle Obama's speechwriter (https://podcasts.apple.com/gb/podcast/sarah-hurwitz-speechwriter-to-the-obamas/id1439875031?i=1000443664935): never say anything to a group of people that you wouldn't say in conversation to one person. Keep your communications straightforward and accessible.

For an analysis of traditional – usually dubbed 'masculine' – illustrations of authority, see Robert Greene's books *The 48 Laws of Power*, *The 33 Strategies of War* and *Mastery* (1998, 2006 and 2012 respectively, all Profile Books). Lots of fascinating examples of how power and confidence have been exerted in the past, not always by the nicest people.

Chapter 1: Be Like the Twenty-First-Century Human You Already Are

For more on William James and 'the restricted circle', see his *Pragmatism and Other Writings* (Penguin Classics, 2000). James's work on 'the social self' and self-esteem, dating from 1890, is a great reminder that our ideas around self-help and self-improvement are not a modern phenomenon. Some of the best self-help books I've read came out years ago but could just as easily be published, and seem fresh and exciting, now, including all of Dorothy Rowe's work, especially *The Successful Self* (HarperCollins, 1983).

If you're interested in reading more about things like the link between the prefrontal cortex and decision-making, I recommend *A Sense of the Self: Memory, The Brain, and Who We Are* by Veronica O'Keane (W. W. Norton & Company, 2021). Not strictly anything to do with neuroscience, two books often return to my thinking when I'm considering how we rate our own behaviour and how we think we come across to others: *Blink: The Power of Thinking Without Thinking* by Malcolm Gladwell (Penguin, 2005) and *Thinking, Fast and Slow* by Daniel Kahneman (Penguin, 2011).

Gallup's 2021 poll on the global mental health crisis (including the 2021 report from the Centers for Disease Control and Prevention): https://www.gallup.com/workplace/357710/next-global-pandemic-mental-health.aspx

The United Nations' 2022 report on making mental health a global priority: https://news.un.org/en/story/2022/10/1129377

2022 interview with Dr Bob Hodges (*Guardian*, 27 November 2022): https://www.theguardian.com/society/2022/nov/27/stress-exhaustion-1000-patients-a-day-english-gp-nhs-collapse

Here's the link to my *How to Own the Room* podcast, with over 150 interviews with (mostly) women talking about their attitudes to confidence, power and public speaking. (Men are allowed in the room too, though – including Google's Matt Brittin, *Succession* actor Brian Cox and pupil referral unit teacher Karl C. Pupé): https://podfollow.com/how-to-own-the-room/view For thoughts on anxiety, uncertainty, resilience and the reinvention of the self, it's worth listening to the interviews on the *How to Own the Room*'s pandemic 'sister podcast' *We Can Rebuild Her*, a series of lockdown conversations about how we manage our confidence during tough times, where I'm talking to people like psychotherapist Julia Samuel and bestselling author (and ex-police office) Clare Mackintosh: https://podfollow.com/we-can-rebuild-her/view

Chapter 2: Be Like a Comedian (Sort Of)

My 2013 book *I Laughed, I Cried: How One Woman Took On Stand-Up and (Almost) Ruined Her Life* (Orion) has a full appendix and reading list on comedy and improvisation courses in London, including Logan Murray's workshops: https://loganmurray.com. I also recommend Logan's book *Be a Great Stand-Up: Teach Yourself* (Teach Yourself, 2010) – relevant and authoritative for anyone who wants more confidence, not just for comedians. *The Serious Guide to Joke Writing: How to Say Something Funny About Anything* by Sally Holloway (Bookshaker, 2010) is excellent, and great for instilling confidence about opening and closing lines.

The original 'bible' about status on stage is Keith Johnstone's *Impro: Improvisation and the Theatre* (Bloomsbury Methuen Drama, 1979). For more on his work, see https://www.keithjohnstone.com/ For more on using high status and happy high status on stage and in improv games based on the work of The Spontaneity Shop (https://www.the-spontaneity-shop.com/), see *The Improv Handbook: The Ultimate Guide to Improvising in Comedy, Theatre, and Beyond* by Tom Salinsky and Deborah Frances-White (Bloomsbury Methuen Drama, 2017), especially pages 93–97 ('High Status Competitions' and 'Happy High Status').

For a completely different take on status and the origins of 'keeping up with the Joneses', see Alain de Botton's *Status Anxiety* (Hamish Hamilton, 2004), a philosophical analysis of why human beings are frequently motivated by wanting to be better and to have more than others.

Chapter 3: Be Like a Wiseguy

Martin Scorsese's tribute to Ray Liotta (*Guardian*, 6 June 2022): https://www.theguardian.com/film/2022/jun/06/martin-scorsese-ray-liotta-goodfellas-gangster-dangerous-disarming-innocent

Aline Santos's interview on the *How to Own the Room* podcast is probably the interview I quote the most frequently. It's such a salient example of a) how many senior women thought that confidence came from behaving like men and b) how quickly that idea has passed out of acceptance. Listen here: https://podfollow.com/how-to-own-the-room/episode/169e60ee4f7347e42af5610d64c8e03030568536/view

One of the most useful sources of insight into high status behaviours and body language comes from the world of conflict negotiation, where every gesture and movement is used for leverage. Priya Parker channels her understanding of this world into our everyday interactions with one another in her book *The Art of Gathering: How We Meet and Why It Matters* (Penguin, 2019). Also recommended: *Never Split the Difference: Negotiating As If Your Life Depended on It* by

Chris Voss with Tahl Raz (Harper Business, 2016) and *You're Not Listening: What You're Missing and Why It Matters* by Kate Murphy (Harvill Secker, 2020).

A sideways take on happy high status in relation to acting and authenticity can be found in *The Method: How the Twentieth Century Learned to Act* by Isaac Butler (Bloomsbury, 2022). This is a wonderful history of method acting, how it has influenced actors' performances and how it affects how we 'read' character on film and television.

Chapter 4: Be Like Final-Scene Sandy and Danny

A lot of my ideas in this chapter are informed by all the reading and thinking I have done over the years about how our childhood and adolescent selves inform the pluses and minuses of our adult selves: how can we max out the pluses and fade away the minuses, without losing who we are? There are two sides to this: one, letting go of outdated or unproven ideas about ourselves or about the world that we formed in childhood; and two, processing and accepting difficult experiences that we had when we were younger. Some books that have helped me think about this: *They F***You Up: How to Survive Family Life* by Oliver James (Bloomsbury, 2002); *The Book You Wish Your Parents Had Read* by Philippa Perry (Penguin Life, 2020); *The Body Keeps the Score: Mind, Brain and Body in the Transformation of Trauma* by Bessel Van Der Kolk (Penguin, 2015).

I also recommend all of Julia Samuels's work on childhood, family and therapy, including her books *Every Family Has a Story: How We Inherit Love and Loss* (Penguin Life, 2022) and *This Too Shall Pass: Stories of Change, Crisis and Hopeful Beginnings* (Penguin Life, 2020) and her podcast *Therapy Works*: https://shows.acast.com/therapy-works

This is a great background read on the making of the movie *Grease* (*Vanity Fair*, 26 January 2016: 'How Grease Beat the Odds and Became the Biggest Movie Musical of the 20th Century'): https://www.vanityfair.com/hollywood/2016/01/grease-movie-musical-john-travolta-olivia-newton-john

The real work of understanding how your confidence was formed and why it might be at a low ebb is done not by reading books or listening to podcasts but in therapy or counselling. If you feel like you need help, a reliable source for finding someone to talk to is https://welldoing.org

Chapter 5: Be Like Clooney on Tequila Duty

Here's chapter and verse on George Clooney's tequila company, Casamigos (*Business Insider*, 23 August 2018): https://www.businessinsider.com/george-clooney-tequila-brand-casamigos-started-by-accident-2017-6?r=US&IR=T

The Clooney story is obviously one about bias. A few recommended reads in relation to sexism: *The Patriarchs: How*

Men Came to Rule by Angela Saini (Fourth Estate, 2023); *Fix the System, Not the Women* by Laura Bates (Simon & Schuster, 2022); *Invisible Women: Exposing Data Bias in a World Designed by Men* by Caroline Criado Perez (Vintage, 2020). In relation to race: *Why I'm No Longer Talking to White People About Race* by Reni Eddo-Lodge (Bloomsbury, 2018); *White Fragility: Why It's So Hard For White People to Talk About Racism* by Robin DiAngelo (Penguin, 2019); *Black and British: A Forgotten History* by David Olusoga (Picador, 2021). And on conflict in the workplace: *Why Men Win at Work* by Gill Whitty-Collins (Luath Press, 2021); *Work Therapy: The Man Who Mistook His Job for His Life – How to Thrive at Work by Leaving Your Emotional Baggage Behind* by Naomi Shragai (W.H. Allen, 2021); and *Jerks At Work: Toxic Coworkers and What to Do About Them* by Tessa West (Ebury Edge, 2022).

Some links to those newspaper headlines if you want to depress yourself further. 'More men called David than women in the shadow cabinet [in 2005]' – this comes from a 2022 article by David Cameron where he talks about his own realization of gender imbalance: https://www.the-times.co.uk/article/david-cameron-we-were-all-white-men-so-i-did-something-about-diversity-xlnnq7sz; 'More men called Dave or Steve [2014]' – from a 2014 report into UKIP election candidates: https://www.indy100.com/news/ukip-has-more-men-called-dave-or-steve-than-it-has-women-7251876; 'More men called Nigel than women [2015]' is from a *New Statesman* report into a

select committee: https://www.newstatesman.com/politics/
2015/07/there-are-more-nigels-women-parliaments-all-
male-all-white-culture-select-committee; 'More men
called David [I missed out Steve here! Sorry, Steve!] than
there are women leading FTSE 100 companies': https://
www.independent.co.uk/news/business/news/women-ftse-
100-gender-discrimination-pay-gap-board-representation-
chief-executive-a8244361.html; 'Men called John [2015]':
https://www.theguardian.com/business/2015/mar/06/johns-
davids-and-ians-outnumber-female-chief-executives-in-
ftse-100 Once you start looking for these examples, there
are so many that you start to go cross-eyed. It goes without
saying that for most of these figures you can replace the
word 'women' with 'ethnic minorities'.

Chapter 6: Be Like a Maverick (Like Cynt)

Some superb reads for thinking about yourself differently, especially in a work context: *You've Been Chosen:
Thriving Through the Unexpected* (Ballantine Books, 2022)
by Cynt Marshall; *Choose Yourself!* by James Altucher
(Lioncrest Publishing, 2013); and *Everything Is Figure-
outable* by Marie Forleo (Penguin, 2019). Also: Seth
Godin's *Poke the Box* (Penguin, 2011) and *The Practice:
Shipping Creative Work* (Penguin Business, 2020), plus
the multiple blog posts Godin has written on 'picking yourself': https://sethgodinwrites.medium.com/pick-
yourself-4b117979d27

Some podcasts (some current, some back-catalogue) I recommend for rethinking work, especially if you are looking to reinvent yourself in some way: *Squiggly Careers* with Sarah Ellis and Helen Tupper: https://podcasts.apple.com/gb/podcast/squiggly-careers/id1202842065; *Creative Rebels* with David Speed and Adam Brazier: https://podcasts.apple.com/gb/podcast/creative-rebels-the-podcast-for-creatives/id1448695774; and *A Bit of Optimism* with Simon Sinek: https://podcasts.apple.com/gb/podcast/a-bit-of-optimism/id1515385282

Esther Perel's work might seem tangential to happy high status as she focuses mostly on relationships, sex and fidelity (or infidelity, depending on how you look at it . . .), but a huge amount of her work is about how comfortably we sit in relation to ourselves, and getting that self-trust in balance before blaming anything that is going wrong in our relationships. Which is a very happy high status (and quietly maverick) thing to do. Recommended: this 2021 TED talk by Perel on routines, rituals and boundaries during stressful times: https://www.ted.com/talks/esther_perel_the_routines_rituals_and_boundaries_we_need_in_stressful_times?language=en

All the social media content from high-energy multi-tasking media entrepreneur Gary Vaynerchuk is a real shot in the arm for anyone who wants maverick happy high status. (I also cited him as a role model for generous happy high status in Chapter 5: this guy ticks a lot of boxes.) Check out his Instagram in particular, where he regularly 'lowers' his status to talk directly to his audience (thereby raising his status). His book on social media, *Jab, Jab, Jab, Right Hook: How to Tell Your Story in a Noisy Social World* (Harper Business, 2013), is amazingly prescient (for a book from 2013) and still the ultimate guide for anyone looking for the confidence to do something bold online.

Chapter 7: Be Like a Dancing Politician

Unsurprisingly, the memoirs of female politicians yield some of the most useful insights into new ways of leadership and/or into overcoming resistance to those new ways. See: *Dear Madam President: An Open Letter to the Women Who Will Run the World* by Jennifer Palmieri (Hodder & Stoughton, 2018) – a behind-the-scenes look at Hillary Clinton's presidential campaign by the former White House communications director; *There Is Nothing For You Here: Finding Opportunity in the Twenty-First Century* by Fiona Hill (Mariner Books, 2021) – in which the foreign policy expert and Trump impeachment witness traces what she has learned from her journey from a working-class background in the north of England to working in the intelligence services in the White House; *Read My Pins: Stories From a Diplomat's Jewel Box* by Madeleine Albright (HarperCollins, 2009) – one of my most treasured second-hand finds, in which the former US secretary of state tells the story of her diplomatic life through the jewellery she wore to some of the most important meetings in history.

Listen to these podcast episodes on *How to Own the Room*: Valerie Jarrett, longest-serving senior adviser to Barack Obama, where she talks about finding her voice and holding her own in difficult situations: https://podfollow.com/ how-to-own-the-room/episode/867826b41b83e3c6afc7bf aa57dcf70c22136f55/view; Anneliese Dodds, first female shadow chancellor of the exchequer: https://podcasts. apple.com/podcast/anneliese-dodds-politician/ id1439875031?i=1000520561391; and – not a politician but with the bearing of one – Indra Nooyi, former CEO of PepsiCo: https://podcasts.apple.com/us/podcast/indra-nooyi-businesswoman/id1439875031?i=1000537176160

This kind of political happy high status is often linked to clarity and excellence in verbal communications, both written and spoken. Great resources for more on developing that: *Connect! How to Inspire, Influence & Energise Anyone, Anywhere, Anytime* by Simon Lancaster (Heligo Books, 2022); *The Art of Speeches and Presentations: The Secrets of Making People Remember What You Say* by Philip Collins (Wiley, 2012) and *She Speaks: Women's Speeches That Changed the World, from Pankhurst to Greta* by Yvette Cooper (Atlantic Books, 2019).

Chapter 8: Be Like a Benched Footballer

Here are the links to my original Instagram posts on the England team's victory: https://www.instagram.com/p/ CgsHPGmIMs_/?igshid=YmMyMTA2M2Y=; and the

German team's defeat – https://www.instagram.com/p/Cgt
Mosbofj7/?igshid=YmMyMTA2M2Y= Not the greatest
sociological experiment of all time but the result still surprised me. We are more open to celebrating great losers
than we think . . .

There are a lot of fantastic books that encourage the link
between sports coaching and life coaching. I avoided these
books for a long time because I thought they were only
relevant for people who wanted to achieve sporting excellence. This was silly of me! There is so much relevant
psychology, even for the most committed armchair dweller.
Some favourites: *Fear Less: How to Win at Life Without Losing Yourself* by Dr Pippa Grange (Vermilion, 2020) – an
examination of failure and resilience by the sports psychologist who coached the 2018 England men's football
squad; *Bounce: The Myth of Talent and the Power of Practice*
by Matthew Syed (Fourth Estate, 2011) – everything you
need to know about the science of sports success from a
table tennis champion turned award-winning writer; *Home
Game: An Accidental Guide to Fatherhood* by Michael Lewis
(Penguin, 2009) – from the author of *Liar's Poker* and *The
Big Short*, this is Lewis's most personal and most 'self-
help' book, telling the story of how understanding sports
coaching helped him become a better person and a better
parent.

There is a whole other book to be written on happy high
status and the psychology of teams and leadership. For
more thinking on how teamwork fits into the picture of

confidence and authenticity, I would recommend: *Turn the Ship Around! A True Story of Building Leaders by Breaking the Rules* by L. David Marquet (Portfolio Penguin, 2013) – a navy officer explains how you get people to do things when they are trapped on a submarine (I really enjoyed reading this and pretending that I would last longer than two seconds in the navy); *Leaders Eat Last: Why Some Teams Pull Together and Others Don't* by Simon Sinek (Penguin, 2017) – from the author of *Start With Why*, this is an obvious recommendation but the title is just so perfect for encapsulating the happy high status idea of being altruistic and putting others first; *Wolfpack: How to Come Together, Unleash Our Power and Change the Game* by Abby Wambach (Piatkus, 2019) – the FIFA World Cup champion on how to incorporate individual power into a team dynamic in work, sport and life.

Tom Daley and 'you're eighteenth-best in the whole country' is from this interview (*Guardian*, 7 October 2021): https://www.theguardian.com/sport/2021/oct/07/tom-daley-on-love-grief-and-health-it-was-hammered-into-me-that-i-needed-to-lose-weight

Chapter 9: Don't Be Like Anyone: Be Like You

On perception of authenticity in public speaking in the *Journal of Learning and Education* (November 2020): https://edulearn.intelektual.org/index.php/EduLearn/article/viewFile/16429/9541

'Could AI Change the Way We Think About Authenticity?', Columbia University ACT Lab, 23 July 2017: https://act-lab.gsb.columbia.edu/research-projects/could-ai-change-way-we-think-about-authenticity

'How Authentic Leaders Communicate', Quantified, 26 October 2017: https://www.quantified.ai/blog/how-authentic-leaders-communicate/ This represents data conducted using artificial intelligence. I was at a presentation by Quantified's CEO and founder Noah Zandan at the 2019 Professional Speechwriters Association annual conference, where he discussed this research in depth. I covered this briefly in a tangential column on the perceptions of class and accents in the *Financial Times* (25 October 2019): https://www.ft.com/content/9835c9ae-f592-11e9-bbe1-4db3476c5ff0

On the effect of our capacity to imagine ourselves in the future: 'Positive Future Time Perspective, PTSD, and Insomnia in Veterans: Do Anger and Shame Keep You Awake?', East Tennessee State University, April 2019: https://dc.etsu.edu/asrf/2019/schedule/107/

One of the best resources for women on authenticity and finding your own path is a book I have recommended repeatedly and which continues to be a source of inspiration, year after year: *Playing Big: For Women Who Want to Speak Up, Stand Out and Lead* by Tara Mohr (Arrow, 2015). (I think anyone could get something out of the exercises in Mohr's book but it is very firmly and unapologetically aimed at women.) For more generally on this topic and for a broader perspective on what we mean by authenticity, I would suggest *Authenticity: How Economics, Evolution and Technology Drive Us to Deceive – and How We Can Fight Back* by Alice Sherwood (Mudlark, 2022).

Chapter 10: Happy High Status For Life

There have been many revisitings of the 1973 'American Fears' study, including this one: 'Is public speaking really more feared than death?', *Communication Research Reports*, April 2012: https://www.researchgate.net/publication/271993200_Is_Public_Speaking_Really_More_Feared_Than_Death The original 1973 study is sometimes referred to as 'The Bruskin Report' or 'The Bruskin Survey'. R.H. Bruskin Associates was a market research company and this particular study used a sample of 3,000 participants.

I'm fascinated by social interactions where we say one thing but mean another. The study I quoted gives an insight into the power dynamics of one part of this: 'Sorry, Not Sorry: The Effect of Social Power on Transgressors' Apology and Nonapology', *Journal of Experimental Psychology: Applied*, January 2022: https://www.researchgate.net/publication/357637069_Sorry_not_sorry_The_effect_of_social_power_on_transgressors'_apology_and_nonapology

I first wrote about the influence my grandparents had on my life in 2006 (*Guardian*, 15 July 2006), shortly after my grandmother's death (my grandad died in 2001): https://www.theguardian.com/lifeandstyle/2006/jul/15/familyandrelationships.family1 It wasn't until many years later that I began to realize that much of their behaviour and attitudes to life coincided perfectly with the idea of happy high status.

Acknowledgements

Books have to be written by writers. But they don't have a shelf life without readers. And sometimes the idea for the book doesn't even exist without readers. I first touched on the theme of happy high status in relation to Michelle Obama in my 2018 book *How to Own the Room: Women and the Art of Brilliant Speaking* (Transworld). Chapter 2 was titled 'Be More Michelle: Inside the World of Happy High Status (also starring George Clooney and the Fly-Catcher)'. As soon as the book came out, this question followed me everywhere: 'Where can I read more about happy high status?' This book is the answer. So, thanks for asking.

To all the readers of *How to Own the Room* and its companion volume *Lift As You Climb*, plus all the listeners of the *How to Own the Room* podcast and everyone who has attended my live events, workshops and seminars over the past five years: I owe you. It was the enthusiasm and curiosity of readers and listeners that encouraged me to sit down and really think about how to define happy high status and explain it to others. Thank you especially to everyone who has taken the time to write a review, send a question or mention these ideas on social media: your questions form the basis of many of the ideas in this book.

The rest of the thinking here has developed by trial and error through my own performing and presenting work, plus through observing others. I'd like to thank the following for all the opportunities they've given me to do that, as well as the friends and supporters who have cheered me on and inspired me with their own confidence: Leo von Bülow-Quirk (who runs my speaker diary); John Gordon and all the team at How To Academy; Isabel Berwick at the *Financial Times*; Eoin O'Callaghan and everyone at Big Fish Films, including the Cigar Club; SMK Campaigners; Jo Stanton and WeSpeak Bermuda; David Murray at the Professional Speechwriters Association; Antti Mustakallio at the Summer School of Rhetoric in Finland; Specialist Speakers; to everyone who works with me in teams and individually. And a special hat-tip to anyone who did anything with me during the lockdowns that gave me a chance to experiment with what happy high status looks like down a desolate laptop camera lens and forced me to confront How to Own the Zoom.

This book was shaped by the enthusiasm of agent Cathryn Summerhayes, a tireless cheerleader of authors and the greatest friend. Thanks also to Jess Molloy in particular, and Curtis Brown more generally, basically for looking after me when I am not always that easy to look after. Editor Lucy Oates at Torva understood the idea for this book immediately and contributed a ton of ideas and suggestions that were immeasurably helpful. It has been a real pleasure working with you, Lucy. For excellent, straightforward design and patience, thanks to Irene

Martínez. Thanks to Alex Newby, Kate Samano and Katrina Whone for making the copy-editing and text design such a delight. I always feel in safe hands with you. Susanna Wadeson and Larry Finlay championed this book from its inception, just as they did with *How to Own the Room* and *Lift As You Climb*. Huge applause to Hannah Winter on the marketing team. To have Alison Barrow working on the PR campaign of a book means you are getting the best of the best – and this one is third time lucky for me so I feel incredibly fortunate. Thank you, AB. You make everything seem easy and worthwhile.

Being an author means owning the tiniest violin in the world because if you have one person who wants to publish you and a few more who want to read you, then, really, you have nothing to complain about ... But it can be stressful, isolating and paranoia-making. So I am really grateful to all the teams at Penguin, Transworld and Torva who really understand and mitigate all the hassle. This book also wouldn't exist without Andrea Henry and Alice Murphy-Pyle, the first readers and champions of *How to Own the Room*.

Thanks, too, to everyone connected to the podcast, especially our executive editor Kate Taylor of Feast Collective, who shaped the vision of it from the start and who was instrumental in our 2021 nomination for Best Business Podcast at the British Podcast Awards. To all the producers who have worked on dozens of episodes: executive producer Ruth Abrahams, Sarah Myles, Sarah Cuddon, Gabriela Jones, Caroline Hughes, Hannah

Varrall, Lynnike Swerts, Lucy Dichmont, Lucy Dearlove, Rich Jarman. You all helped me to sound happy high status even when I was not. Thanks to David Hepworth who gave us a shout-out in the *Radio Times* at a critical moment.

Endless gratitude to our first podcast sponsor, Katy Cole at knowledge consultancy Spoken, who kept us on our feet through more than a dozen podcast series and was an endless source of encouragement and insight. Katy, I can't thank you enough for all your support: you made this happen. Thank you to all our brilliant guests who have given their time and insight so generously, creating this incredible audio archive resource on women and public speaking, which I hope will be available for years to come. Special mention goes to Mary Portas, who casually said yes to an interview before the podcast even existed, thereby bringing the podcast into existence. That was a text worth sending.

Thank you also to everyone – oh yes, this is important! – who has said 'no' to the podcast. I've been turned down by dozens of household names, including BAFTA and Oscar winners who say, without fail, 'You know, Viv . . . I can't talk to you for that podcast because I don't know how to own the room. I mean, who would want to listen to me?' You are why this project continues: because you are the daily reminder to me that no one feels confident, no one feels on top of their nerves, everyone thinks everyone else is more happy high status than they are. And, no, I will never say who is on the 'no' list. Because I hope one day they will change their minds. The whole point of talking about these things is to talk about the resistance.

I owe a huge debt to Alex MacLaren of The Spontaneity Shop, a brilliant coach, superb director and excellent human being who first planted the seed of the idea for this book when I signed up to a course with him in 2011. Ancient thanks also to all the improvisers I knew around that time: Simon Lukacs and the 2012–14 cast of the Edinburgh Fringe show *Upstairs Downton* (a real testing ground for status); everyone who went on to found The Free Association (another brilliant place for improv workshops); to Cariad Lloyd and everyone in *Austentatious*; to everyone at the Bath Literature Festival I worked with from 2012 to 2016, when I was forming a lot of the ideas that eventually made their way into this book and I was truly capable of boring anyone stupid about happy high status and 'the sacred bond between audience and performer'. (Apologies especially to Alex Clark for that one.)

For generalized, non-specific support whose effect is easily underestimated: Jane Lindsey, Natasha Musson, Laura Kenyon, Nicola Waite, Fiona Grundy, Caitlin McAllister (for social media support), Sean Brightman (who does my website and all my non-publishing design work), Suzanne Azzopardi, Lucy Porter, Kira Cochrane, Greer Duru, Julia Hornsby, Maura Wilding, Sadie Jones, Dixi Stewart, Maggie Tibble, Louise Barfield, Hatty Ashdown, Gill Whitty-Collins, J. Luxembourg, Christobel Kent, Charlotte Wood, Sarah Hurwitz, Claire Locher, Gita Ramakrishnan, Ninja Struye de Swielande, Bella von

Ribbentrop, Isabelle Gaudeul-Ehrhart. For all my swim buddies who give me a break from talking about all this stuff and only want to talk about bobble hats: you know who you are. And a shout-out to my oldest friends Claire, Dawn, Jen, Lucie and Susan, in careful alphabetical order: you keep me on the straight and narrow. Extra applause to Stephen Barber, who facilitated all of this work in the first place after we first got into a conversation about clowning while waiting for a train in Suffolk.

This is the sixth book overseen by Ola Majerz as well as by Simon, Vera, Jack and (currently in absentia) Will. You are all naturally happy high status and I'm always playing catch-up. If anything, I have become more petty with each subsequent book, so thank you for your tolerance, which seems to expand to fit. At least with this one I actually did the writing at home instead of melodramatically sequestering myself in various unpredictable hermit-like locations, having finally understood it's not very happy high status to be a diva. As Billy Crystal as Harry (a happy high status case study if ever there was one) says in *When Harry Met Sally*: 'I feel like I'm growing.'

Viv Groskop is an award-winning writer, stand-up comedian, playwright, and TV and radio presenter. She is the host of the podcast *How to Own the Room*, the biggest audio resource in the world on women and public speaking and in the top 1 per cent of podcasts globally, with over two million downloads. *How to Own the Room* podcast guests have included Hillary and Chelsea Clinton, Margaret Atwood, Professor Mary Beard, Nigella Lawson, and very occasionally a man (such as Brian Cox, *Succession*'s Logan Roy). Viv started her comedy career by doing one hundred gigs on one hundred consecutive nights in her late thirties, when she had three children under the age of seven, and went on to perform six years of sell-out one-woman shows at the Edinburgh Fringe. Her previous books include *How to Own the Room: Women and the Art of Brilliant Speaking* and *Lift As You Climb: Women, Ambition and How to Change the Story*. As a performance coach, she works with women and senior teams in business and media, helping them to redefine leadership and authority – and generally to worry less about how they come across, so they can just do their work.

How to Own the Room: Women and the Art of Brilliant Speaking

Viv Groskop

Most books about public speaking don't tell you what to do when you open your mouth and nothing comes out. And they don't tell you how to get over the performance anxiety that most people naturally have. They don't tell you what to do in the moments when, as a woman, you are made to feel small. They don't tell you how to own the room. This book does.

How to Own the Room explores the presence, performance and authenticity of recent history's great women speakers, and reveals what they do when they deliver those game-changing moments, so that you can apply their qualities to your own life. From great political leaders and stand-up comedians to campaigners and feminists, this powerful book shows what happens when women find their voice.

'Demystifies the art of talking to people' *The Times*

'This book is going to help so many people. It's brilliant' Emma Gannon

Life As You Climb: Women and
the Art of Ambition

Viv Groskop

They say there's a special place in hell for
women who don't support other women. But
what does the idea of 'sisterhood' really look like?
How do you put it into action? What can you do
to make things better for others? And how do
you do that without disadvantaging yourself?

Part self-help guide, part masterclass in survival
skills for life and work, *Lift As You Climb* is a book
about all those moments when you're not quite sure
how far to assert yourself. It's the ultimate confidence
bible for women who want to go after what they want,
but not at someone else's expense. And it addresses
one of the biggest issues women face in the
workplace – how to be ambitious without
losing your sense of self.

Full of tips, takeaways and useful insights,
Lift As You Climb tells you everything you need
to know about making life better for yourself
without making it worse for others.

'Empowering' Elizabeth Day

'A book to have at your side for
any situation' Mary Portas